MONDAY
MORNING
LEADERSHIP
for Women

Valerie Sokolosky

CornerStone
Leadership Institute

www.**cornerstoneleadership**.com

MONDAY MORNING LEADERSHIP
for Women

CornerStone Leadership Institute
P.O. Box 764087
Dallas, TX 75376
888.789.LEAD

Printed in the United States of America
ISBN: 0-9719424-7-1

Credits

Editors	Alice Adams
	Sue Coffman
Design, art direction, and production	Back Porch Creative

This book is dedicated to the thousands of
successful people who invest time sharing
their experiences and mentoring others.
May the words captured on these pages help
you to learn faster and enjoy life's journey more.

MONDAY MORNING LEADERSHIP
for Women

Table of Contents

Prologue

*H*ow could my career and personal life go from dizzying heights to downward spiral in a matter of months?

That is a question that I had to be painfully honest with myself to answer a couple of years ago. And you're about to find out how my career and personal life swerved off course and what I did to get back on track.

My name is Taylor Grant, and one of the greatest discoveries of my life was finding a mentor who could guide me through the stormy seas just when things seemed to be swirling out of control.

Not too long ago, I felt on top of the world. I was a newly promoted manager — confident I would skyrocket to the top of our organization. After all, before my promotion, my own performance had been stellar. I hate to brag, but I was recognized as a rising star. When a management job became available, I was ready. Everyone seemed to think that I was the obvious choice to lead others because of my personal success.

At first, my team could do no wrong. Management seemed a natural transition for me...or maybe it was just beginner's luck. Regardless of the reason, we were accomplishing our goals. The team seemed to respond to me, and everyone was enjoying working with each other. Great things were happening in my career.

My marriage to Michael was bliss. We finally had time for each other and our two little guys, Mason and Josh. In the evenings, we played games or rode bikes in the neighborhood. We enjoyed going to the lake on the weekends and just being together. Picnics, baseball, swimming — it didn't matter what we did. It was all fun, and life was good!

But then things began changing that affected everything in my life.

Business slowed to a crawl, and productivity started to drag bottom. Competition got tougher, and pressure to perform was stronger than ever. All of a sudden, my team was not responding to me. It seemed as though the honeymoon was over and reality had hit.

I was struggling to keep the team focused and productive in an economy that was whipping like a flag in a hurricane. Upper management seemed to change directions as often as the gale, creating choppy economic seas around us.

Our changing work schedules began to include Saturdays at least twice a month. Our once-a-month meetings exploded into once-a-week meetings. Conflicting priorities were frustrating to my team and me.

As a manager, I felt responsible and a little guilty for the turmoil experienced by the team members. After all, they all have families, too. There were rumors of pay cuts and even layoffs. You can imagine what that did to the team's motivation. I was worried that they would all look for other jobs, and I would be left with no one on the team.

I was starting to feel like part of the problem as I struggled to figure out ways I could be part of the solution.

Naturally, the problems at work spilled over to my time at home. My job, my schedule and my stress level played havoc with my family life. Even the boys seemed out of sorts and could tell that all was not well with their mom.

Michael, my patient husband, had always been there to encourage me, so I hated bringing my woes home. I knew he had his own business issues, since his industry has been riding the economic roller coaster as well.

Stress was mounting for both of us.

Michael and I had decided long ago that our children would be raised with both of us sharing the responsibilities. We both enjoyed family activities like attending the boys' soccer games, and we would do everything we could to avoid missing a match, even as our business lives become more demanding. Frankly, I was beginning to feel guilty. I worried that I may not be the "mom" I intended to be. I worried I was not carrying my load.

One more thing I thought I was learning: Being able to successfully balance your life is a myth. It was definitely not MY reality.

As a woman, I felt overwhelmed, trying to do a good job at work and still maintain the family life I wanted and had dreamed about my whole life. I needed someone to talk to — someone unbiased who understood what it is like to wear so many hats all at one time.

Michael is a great listener, and I value his opinion. But he just can't understand what it's like to be in my shoes now — to feel responsible for so many people, so many futures, and so many details. Sure, he sympathizes, and that's great, but I needed someone who had been there and done that. I needed someone who would shoot straight with me about whether I really have what it takes to move ahead in my job.

One more thing: Staying home has never been an option for me because of my competitive nature.

I was frustrated, to say the least. Thank goodness for my daily exercise routine and a yoga class during the lunch hour to relieve tension. Not only did I dump stress in that class, but there I also found my soon-to-be mentor and friend.

Suzanne Chambers is well known in our area as a highly successful business executive with a large architectural firm. She is also a fundraiser extraordinaire and someone who is active on the social scene, although it is usually in conjunction with one of her charities. Her genuine smile is seen regularly in the newspaper and at events all over the city.

Success has not come easily for Suzanne. A single mom who raised a son on her own to become a thriving adult, she began her career as a secretary to the owner of the firm. Early on, her boss saw her potential and pushed her career to what is now a full-partner position. In her high-profile role, Suzanne recently guided the firm through a complex –but successful merger. The newspapers featured her in numerous articles. Just last month I read that she had been honored for her volunteer work at Goodwill Industries and St. Jude's Children's Research Hospital.

Suzanne is definitely a woman to be admired.

On my first day at Wednesday yoga class, Suzanne welcomed me with her engaging smile and a friendly toss of her head. As soon as I heard her name, I remembered reading about her. Here I was, talking with her as if we had known each other for years, not minutes. She was as lovely in person as she was in the press. She was everything you would think of as a role model for successful women — polished and professional.

Suzanne seemed to carry herself confidently but without arrogance. She was strong without trying to be a male stereotype. She was also known to be a formidable competitor in the boardroom and yet cared deeply about her people.

As the class progressed, I was impressed by Suzanne's ability to connect with people. She simply had a gift for communicating easily with everyone. Although she could have intimidated every other person in the class, she made us feel at ease.

As the weeks went by, I talked more often with Suzanne. I shed some of my stress in class, but I continued struggling with questions about my leadership capabilities. At work, we just weren't getting the results we needed, and every member of the team was just as concerned and pressured as I was.

The questions and doubts were haunting. What if I was good alone but was just not management material? Was I meant to lead a team? What if the economy stayed in a slump for more than a few months or quarters?

One day at yoga, after I had spent a restless night worrying, Suzanne noticed the bags under my eyes and asked, "Taylor, did you pull an all-nighter? You look worn out."

By this time we had known each other at yoga long enough to chat about something more than the weather or children. Almost relieved, I began pouring out my concerns.

"Suzanne, I don't know how to begin," I stammered. "I'm confused and worried. Maybe this job is too big for me. I just can't seem to get my act together like I used to. And all I do is work.

"The boys are saying, 'Mom, why don't you have time to play with us anymore?' Honestly, by the time I get home, all I want to do is crash. This management thing is just not what it's cracked up to be. This isn't working out like I thought it would."

She listened as I gushed. "I'm sorry to hear all this, Taylor. What can I do to help? After all, I've been in your shoes, and it's not easy to be 'superwoman.' I sense that's what you're trying to be."

How did she know? That's exactly how I felt. But I was uncomfortable talking to someone as successful as she was.

"Suzanne, I really appreciate your asking. Look, I know you have an extremely busy schedule, so I wouldn't want to take up too much of your time with my problems," I said.

She was quick to reply, "I wouldn't have offered if I hadn't meant it! Actually, I enjoy sharing any lessons in business or in life because I've had to learn most of them the hard way. And if I can help you bypass some of the pitfalls that caused me to stumble along the way, that's my reward. I get excited watching others succeed."

"Wow. I'd be grateful for any help you could give me. Where would we start?"

"Well, let's set some ground rules," Suzanne said.

Uh, oh...here it comes, I thought. This *was* too good to be true.

"It's going to take a significant time commitment on both our parts," she outlined aloud, "and the best time for me to meet with you would be Monday mornings. In fact, that's the only free time I have right now. How would Mondays work for you?"

"Great. Monday morning meetings would be a great way to begin each week," I responded.

Suzanne's additional suggested parameters included the following:

1. We would meet for an hour before work.

2. Starbucks was an appropriate place to meet, since it was about halfway between our homes.

3. Eight weeks seemed to be a realistic time frame for what Suzanne wanted to accomplish.

4. We agreed not to discuss Monday-morning meeting material or results during yoga, a time we needed to unwind and decompress.

5. I would take action each week and try to improve situations we identified that were giving me particular heartburn.

6. Suzanne agreed to mentor me only if I promised to take what I learned and share it with others. After our meetings concluded, I would teach others my leadership lessons and help them become leaders in their own right.

That was too easy. I couldn't believe this role model for women in our community was offering to take me on, to help me solve some of the problems I encountered, and to be my mentor.

Nothing could have been more exciting at the moment. I was eager to get started.

"Let's do it, Suzanne. I'm ready and willing if you are." I beamed with anticipation.

Suzanne seemed equally enthusiastic about this new project. "Well, more than a few years ago, someone stepped up to the plate to help me through a difficult period. They held my hand and made me not only a better businessperson but also a better person. In return for this huge gift, they asked only that I pass on what I had learned. So now it's my turn to be the mentor and your turn to pass on the lessons," she explained.

Those eight sessions led to a turnaround in my career and my family life. As you read my story, perhaps you also can glean a few tips that will help you in your journey.

This is my commitment to Suzanne: to share Lessons Learned and thus to pass them on.

The First Monday

From Steamroller to Leader

*A*fter a relaxing weekend and lots of fun with the family, Monday morning came all too quickly. I worried the night before. Had I made a mistake in committing to these sessions? What if Suzanne viewed me as some idiot without the necessary skills to manage my team? Even as I was wondering whether I really had the tools for success, another voice reminded me how fortunate I was to have such an amazing mentor who had offered to help.

"Oh, well, here goes," I thought as I parked my car at Starbucks.

As I walked among the scattering of Monday-morning coffee drinkers sitting around small round tables inside, the air had that distinct aroma of freshly ground coffee beans. The atmosphere was inviting. This obviously popular place had all the customary goodies — music playing, with the CDs for purchase; shelves of tempting munchies to go with the coffees; and too many choices of paraphernalia like bottles and coffee machines.

I looked around while waiting for my latte and picked up a couple of finger puppets for my kids. That old guilt feeling was hitting me again — and it was not quite 8 a.m. Even as I paid for the puppets, I realized I was buying them because I felt guilty that I was not spending enough time with Mason and Josh.

Suzanne had already captured the inviting overstuffed chairs in the corner. Perfect! Away from the crowd so we could talk openly. She looked up and waved at me. "I have the seats," she said. "Grab your coffee and we'll get going."

Settling into the comfy brown chair, I pulled out a pen and turned to a new sheet in my planner to capture what we discussed. Suzanne's warm smile made me feel at ease.

"I really like that you're prepared to take notes," she said, gesturing in my direction. "It's hard to remember everything that's said at meetings; at least it is for me. Having a planner and a place to keep the notes you're taking is a great idea, Taylor," Suzanne added as she took her own planner from her briefcase. "So what do you want to talk about this morning?"

"Suzanne," I blurted out readily, "what's the secret to being a good leader? Is there a secret formula? Do most leaders do things a certain way that works? Maybe that's too general a question, but it can't be as difficult as I'm making it. Every morning I wake up thinking what I could do differently to be more effective as a manager. Does this make sense, or am I just rambling?"

"Those are pretty heady questions," Suzanne teased. "Let me take another sip of coffee." She smiled, studying her perfectly manicured nails for a moment before answering.

"Taylor, I think you're trying to make this too difficult," she began, looking me squarely in the eyes. "So much of being a good leader is common sense. Then again, being a good leader is not easy. You know the saying: 'If common sense is so common, why don't more people have it?'

"Now, to answer your question about a secret formula for successful leadership — if one exists, I haven't found it. As far as doing things a certain way, I can only share what I personally do and what is being done by other leaders I admire."

"Okay, I'm all ears," I said.

"Let's start by looking first at what leadership is and what it is not. It's really pretty simple. **Leadership is influencing others to follow.** After all, if you don't have followers, you're not leading anyone. So in my opinion, leadership is about working with and relating to people.

Leadership is not something that I…or anyone else…can give you. You can't buy it. And you can't expect others to anoint you with leadership just because you're the manager. Leadership has to be earned. The long and short of it…it takes time."

She sat back in the chair, relaxed and then continued.

"One of the things I've observed from leaders I admire is that the person creates positive change and influences people to move in a new direction. If you'll take just a minute, I'll bet you can think back on a new direction for your team that you've influenced since you became a manager, Taylor. Did you get people on board relatively easily, or was it like pulling teeth?" she teased again.

"I think I'm pretty good at getting people on board, but you're right. At first, some things were sort of like pulling teeth," I said, remembering back. "The first week I was promoted, we were asked to develop a customer-satisfaction survey and get it completed within two months.

"I noticed that my team was not getting into this assignment because they were concentrating on their regular tasks and saw developing the survey as a diversion. So I created a competition where I divided them into work teams to develop ideas for the survey. I had a small reward for the winning team. It was interesting to see how everyone really wanted to win…even for a small insignificant prize. The bottom line was that we got the survey results ahead of schedule. I guess that *was* influencing, wasn't it?"

"You bet that was," Suzanne said. "And you showed leadership without using your title. Good for you. Some people have the misconception that leadership is based on position alone. There's a great quote that says, 'It's not the position that makes the leader; it's the leader that makes the position.' Having a title doesn't automatically make a person a good leader."

I couldn't have agreed more. A serious expression replaced Suzanne's familiar smile as she went on.

"Here's another misconception. Some people believe that leadership automatically comes with intelligence. That's not true, either. We all know brilliant thinkers who lack the ability to lead. So leadership is *not* based on IQ. Entrepreneurs can be assumed to be good leaders. Again, it's not always the case. I saw this firsthand.

"One of my high school classmates earned a Ph.D. and became a successful writer. Once her writing began getting attention, she started a management-development organization. Things went well for a while, as long as people were buying her books. But she led by her position, not by influencing others. In fact, people were afraid of her. They did what they were told to do, but nothing more. In time, the good people left. She did nothing to build loyalty and certainly didn't instill passion for the business in the workers who stayed on.

"In the long run, neither being an entrepreneur and CEO of her company nor having a high IQ made her an effective leader. The sad thing is, her organization suffered, and most of her people either left or were fired. She's almost back to where she started."

"That's a bummer," I said. "With all her potential, I wonder why she didn't see the handwriting on the wall and make alterations."

"If we could get inside people's heads, we wouldn't be sitting here today," Suzanne answered. "But to understand the attributes of a good leader, we have to begin by looking at where leadership starts. People are *not* born leaders. Leadership is learned and developed. It starts way back in our early lives with who we are as individuals. Now, don't be misled. I'm not saying find a couch and let's discuss psychology 101."

We both laughed.

She went on to explain her views: "**Leadership depends on what we've learned from the people and the experiences that have shaped our values and our character.** Then it's how we apply those influences into unique points of view and behaviors that counts."

Then she asked a question. "Can you think back to people and events that impacted you and made you the person you are today?"

"Hmmm. Now let *me* take that sip of coffee." It was my turn to hesitate before speaking.

"My dad is the one who first comes to mind," I offered. "He had a major impact on my life. I remember his saying, 'Think before you speak.' I was the talker in the family, and sometimes I'd blurt out something that hurt my little sister's feelings or came across as rude to someone. Come to think of it, I do use his advice today. In fact, I now find myself saying the very same thing to our boys. Isn't it funny how we pass on those childhood messages to our children?"

"That's a good point, Taylor. In fact, let me show you something." She tore a piece of paper out of her planner and drew a picture something like this:

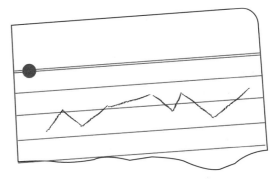

"We've all had ups and downs in our lives," she explained as her pencil traced the jagged line she had drawn. "The values and character that leaders demonstrate in day-to-day business are influenced by those ups and downs and the people involved — some are positive and some are negative. What matters is that you reflect on these experiences and people and what you learned from them.

"So the first thing you've got to do is to become aware of the events and people in your past that have influenced you and the leadership lessons you learned from these experiences.

"What you just told me is that you've learned to think before you speak, which is definitely a leadership trait. You're really talking about being a good listener. That reminds me of something my grandmother always said: 'We have two ears and only one mouth for a reason.' Right, Taylor?"

She smiled.

"I have a suggestion for this week. Give some thought to what we've talked about today. I think this has been a good beginning, a great grounding conversation that will serve as a foundation for anything you will encounter as a manager. Now, take time this week to note the people and events that have shaped your behavior as a leader. Then figure out where those positive traits came from. I'll bet you'll be surprised at what you'll remember."

She drew this picture as an illustration:

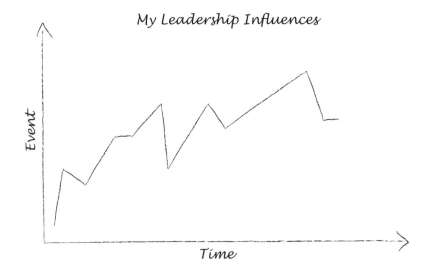

As she sketched, I wondered what some of her lows and highs were and what lessons these events had contributed to her leadership style.

"What about you, Suzanne? Any stories about how you operate today based on what you've learned?"

"Certainly, Taylor. Leadership has to be earned, as I said before. See that dip right there?" She pointed to the paper. "In my experience, I've watched newly promoted managers —particularly women — try too hard to prove themselves too quickly. They go overboard to show they are worthy of the promotion. They try to be the be-all and end-all.

"Here's my personal example. In my first job, I worked for a man who taught me a lot. I was so passionate about my job that I put high energy into every little thing. The intensity around me must have been tremendous. I was a go, go, go kind of girl who wanted everyone to get on board and move — move as fast as I was moving — and I had no tolerance for people who didn't show the same energy. I made fast decisions without asking for input from anyone. After all, wasn't that what a manager should be — decisive?

"One day my boss gave me some good advice I practice today. He said, 'Suzanne, you can be intense in every part of your role, or you can choose to spend your energy where it counts. Just know that the perception you're creating is that you're a steamroller. People don't feel they have a voice. You come across too strongly. You can't force your ideas on others. You've got to let them think they can give *you* ideas and that you will listen.'

"I never forgot that lesson, and today I try very hard to have an open mind. I've been delighted with ideas others have brought to me, and those are the ones that actually create excitement for all of us. To use 'management speak,' you can't 'sell through'; you have to get 'buy-in.' "

Then she added the box below to capture the lessons that had been learned at these points:

Lessons Learned that Define Who I Am As a Leader

1.
2.
3.
4.
5.
6.
7.

I took the paper, clipped it into my organizer in my "things to do" file and thanked her for a great first Monday-morning session as we started toward the door.

Putting on her sunglasses, Suzanne smiled and said, "I'll look forward to seeing these filled in. See you next Monday, Taylor. Have a good one."

No sooner had I arrived at my desk than there was an e-mail from Suzanne that read:

Good Luck

From: Suzanne Chambers
Date: Monday, October 20
To: Taylor Grant
Subject: Good Luck

Taylor:

Good luck this week looking at your leadership traits and where they came from. Right now you have a great opportunity to demonstrate your leadership capabilities. That's why you've been given this role. It's not about the title. It's about a reputation. And that comes with time. So be patient. I'll be looking forward to seeing you next Monday and hearing how the week went.

Suzanne

It was exhilarating to know how sincere she was about mentoring me. I had a lot to learn and was excited — not just excited, but also energized about the journey. Patience, I reminded myself!

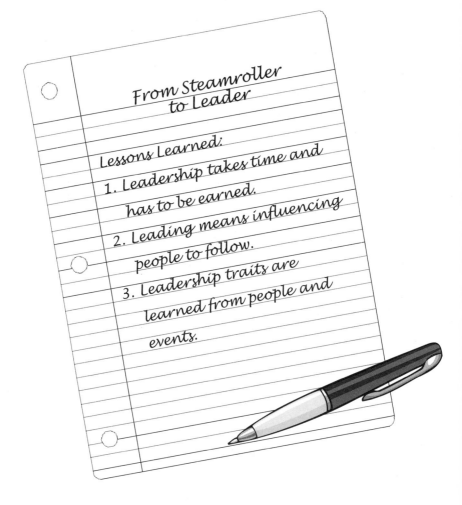

From Steamroller
to Leader

Lessons Learned:
1. Leadership takes time and has to be earned.
2. Leading means influencing people to follow.
3. Leadership traits are learned from people and events.

The Second Monday

Rocks, Pebbles, Sand and Water

Monday morning. The alarm clock lulled me out of my sleepy consciousness with lilting music from my favorite jazz station. I swung my legs over the side of the bed and planted my feet, ready to start the week.

Here's the routine at my house: I cook breakfast for Mason and Josh while Michael dresses them for school. Mason is our active little first-grader, and Josh is a precocious third-grader with questions about everything. Just like me, I thought as I stirred up eggs for their favorite, French toast.

After breakfast, Michael secured them in the car, ready for school. Kissing them all goodbye, I drove to my second Monday-morning meeting with Suzanne.

This past week had been eventful, so I had lots to share with her. As I drove up to Starbucks, I saw Suzanne through the plate glass window, standing in line ready to order.

As I walked up to join her, she nodded, "Hey there, Taylor. How did last week go? Any discoveries from your leadership exercise?"

We paid the cashier, grabbed our coffees and lemon bars, and settled into two overstuffed chairs that seemed to be waiting just for us.

"Absolutely," I said as I pulled out my piece of paper to show her what I had filled in. "It's true what you said about how my behaviors have been formed from experiences and people."

Here's what I wrote:

Leadership Influences and Lessons Learned

1. **Lead in sixth-grade play**
   I learned I had no problem being in front of an audience and actually had fun getting attention.

2. **Moved away**
   I learned not to depend on only one group of people for friendship. I had to make new friends and did so easily.

3. **Junior class president**
   This was my first leadership role, and it taught me how to influence people by working with them. We all had a great time because we got along so well. It was a lesson about the importance of teamwork, since there's no way I could have simply told that group what to do.

4. Got loan, went to college, excelled

Here was a really important lesson. I had to think outside the box and figure out how to get the money to go to college. Not going wasn't an option for me. I was a solid performer, determined to further my education. With the help of a loan and a job on campus selling advertising for the school paper, I was able to get through college.

5. First job with a great boss

Mr. Mateja was the kind of boss who let me spread my wings and try new skills. As long as I performed, he was willing to support me in doing new projects. I learned to take risks, to try out different ideas.

6. Met Michael and married

I've learned to multitask. After the children came along, some things don't get done as well as I'd like, but I've learned to relax my perfectionism.

7. First promotion to management

What I am now learning is that although past successes have been rewarded with this promotion, I have new skills and theories to learn in order to become an effective leader.

Suzanne studied my completed assignment carefully as she drank her coffee and ate her lemon bar.

I explained that my lessons had been mostly from people and events outside my family. My parents' divorce led me to be fairly independent at an early age, taking on certain responsibilities much sooner than some of my friends.

My mom and stepfather had careers in retail. Both worked long hours and rarely came to any of my activities. My mom, of course, gave me love and encouragement, but along the way I gained self-confidence through excelling in my classes and extracurricular activities. Popularity in school also served me well, and I learned to be competitive early on.

I explained the highs and lows on my paper to Suzanne and how they impacted me. Admittedly, I had learned lessons I had never looked at in terms of leadership. Now I saw the connection, and it was exciting. Obviously, I was ready for more.

Suzanne seemed pleased. "Good for you. It's kind of fun to see how you've grown through the years, isn't it? It's also clear that you're a determined woman who doesn't know how to spell failure." Suzanne smiled again. "So what's on your mind for this morning?"

Last week had been a killer. My team had worked hard to get some critical issues handled. Our competition had been eating our lunch lately, which had us scrambling. Come to think of it, this team is always in perpetual motion. It's the only way we know how to work. But it often seemed to me that we were just spinning our wheels.

Sooner or later I knew we'd reach a point where we couldn't work any harder. Then what? Maybe Suzanne could give me a few pointers. Overtime was skyrocketing, and my budget was at the breaking point. I needed to get a handle on how to work smarter, not harder.

"It's about how hard we're all working," I began, "yet we're not getting everything done. We're putting in more hours, but it feels like we're accomplishing less. I've got to find ways to work smarter before we all burn out and before our spouses get frustrated and leave us all. It's a hectic pace involving a lot of overtime hours, Suzanne. I wish I could give them some relief, and I would if I knew how." My frustration was showing.

My mentor put her coffee cup down and stared into it as if she saw something from the past. "I'm reminded of a game I used to play with my two older brothers when I was a little girl. We loved to play in the sandbox with rocks and dirt. My mother would fuss at me because she didn't think little girls were supposed to get *that* dirty."

The grin playing at the corners of Suzanne's mouth indicated this was a special memory.

"I can relate," I replied. "Mason and Josh used to spend hours in the sandbox Michael built in our backyard. I kept it filled with plastic toys and trucks. They loved it. And who cares how dirty they got? Boys will be boys, right?" I laughed and wondered where she was going with this illustration.

Suzanne continued, "So picture this — your boys get big rocks from your yard, and they fill an empty plastic jar to the top, stuffing as many rocks as possible into that jar. Then one of them dumps some pebbles in and shakes the jar, causing the pebbles to work down into the spaces between the big rocks.

"Then they start dumping sand in, and it goes into the space between the rocks and the pebbles. It's getting really heavy, but the game goes on. Amazing how much sand gets in and around the pebbles and rocks until it too comes to the top. Finally they add water.

"Once again, the jar is filled to the brim." Suzanne paused. "Now hang on. There's a good story here about where to spend your time so you won't get burned out.

"The jar is your day, and it's filled with all kinds of activities and demands. We all have big rocks we have to fit into that jar every day. Those rocks are your large priorities that must get done. So you have to decide what your big rocks are for the day. Those are the jobs, the responsibilities you get paid to do, and the activities your organization views as important and necessary to meet the goals and responsibilities you're measured on in your performance reviews. When time is short, you can't take these rocks out.

"The pebbles represent what you enjoy doing. Since you're a people person, Taylor, those are probably the times you interact with your team or make phone calls to clients. The sand stands for those details you *have* to do in your job, like fill out reports or solve customer complaints. And the water — that's clutter that gets in everywhere!"

Demands? Clutter? Suzanne had definitely captured my attention!

"None of these are bad," Suzanne continued. "We need the gamut — from the large projects to those times we need rest — that's what keeps us stimulated and adds excitement to our lives. The key is balance and fitting in each of these categories where they're supposed to be."

I liked her analogy. It was clear and simple.

"Okay," I said eagerly. "I buy all that, and it makes perfect sense. Besides balancing these parts of my day, what else can I do differently? One thing is for sure. More of the same is giving me more of the same. If you can help me with this, you'll be a Houdini. I'm fresh out of ideas."

My mentor brought our focus back to the subject. "I didn't mean to make it sound easy, Taylor, but it's not magic, either. It's getting clear on what various parts in your day look like and then knowing how to redistribute them. We all have more work to do these days and fewer resources.

"Unfortunately, that probably won't change in our lifetimes, but maybe we can take it one step at a time. You know the old saying that goes, 'Inch by inch, it's a cinch?' " Suzanne smiled. I was beginning to notice her clever use of these standard old truisms.

"First, who's in control of your time?" she asked.

"Me, of course!"

"Yes, and that goes for each person on your team. The hard part is to take that control seriously." Her voice was gentle but firm.

"Have you ever kept track of how many phone calls or interruptions you get daily? If you have, that's a start. It was always the case that when I needed to focus on something, the phone rang or someone stopped by my office. But if you're under the gun with a deadline, hold your calls and close the door.

"Get your team to recognize that **when your door is closed, you need to be left alone.** I personally hate to have my door closed, but sometimes I have to close it out of necessity. As for the team, since they don't have offices, have them hang red ribbons outside their cubes, and let others know the red ribbons mean DO NOT DISTURB! It may sound silly, but if everyone knows the signals, it will work if you stick to it!" Suzanne sounded confident.

"It's worth a try. Why not?" I answered my own question. "We have to do something different, and that's definitely a starting point. By the way, have you heard the definition of insanity?" It was my turn to give her a quote. "Insanity is doing the same thing over and over and expecting different results." We both chuckled.

"Okay," I continued, "so we all might be able to **take more control of our time by limiting distractions.** Now, what about meeting schedules? It often seems as if we go from one meeting or conference call to another."

"Are these meetings all necessary, Taylor? Could some of them be handled individually rather than as a group?" Suzanne asked such obvious questions.

"Here's what I've observed in other companies. If they schedule Wednesday-afternoon meetings, they have them — whether they need to meet or not. People take their time to meet but leave the meeting with no new information, no new insights. Meetings like these — for meeting's sake — are time-wasters and contribute nothing to the bottom line!" Suzanne was emphatic.

"I would say very few employees like to be taken away from accomplishing the critical things that need to be done just so they could attend a mandatory meeting. So now you're the manager. When should you ask your team members to interrupt their schedules for a meeting?"

I was already looking back at some of the unnecessary meetings I had called.

"If you're an effective manager, it's up to you to hold only those meetings that are absolutely necessary, meetings that give your team something to make their jobs easier or tips to make them more effective employees. One way to accomplish this is to **eliminate meetings that aren't contributing to the bottom line and then *stick to it*.**

"These days, nobody has time to waste, especially waiting for everybody to show up for meetings. To encourage prompt attendance, I would **set specific time allocations for meetings and** *stick to them*," Suzanne continued. "Reward those who arrive on time by starting and stopping the meetings on schedule. If people are late, make them responsible for catching up on what they missed — after the meeting. **Have a formal agenda and** *stick to it.* Appoint a time manager to monitor the time, and *stick to your schedule.*

"One more tip — your attendance isn't always required. These days, managers are often involved in so many meetings that they have little time to spend with their teams, so if it's a company meeting for information purposes only, delegate down and send someone to the meeting in your place. **You don't need to be at every meeting.**

"By incorporating these time-management steps into how you manage your team, you'll soon earn a reputation for being crisp and focused. There are only so many hours in the day, so be selfish with your time. Don't let others consume it," Suzanne emphasized.

I was writing everything down, even things I knew were common sense. It's one thing to know some of this intuitively. It's another thing to "stick to it." Being consistent — that was the common thread.

Suzanne was on a roll. "Here's an idea that's outside the box," she said. "**Stand up during meetings.** They'll end in thirty minutes. I guarantee it. That's a trick my boss taught me, and it works. No one wants to stand for long meetings," she chuckled. "People will get the point."

"Do you mean have the leader of the meeting stand — or have everyone stand?" I asked, a little sheepishly, because I was getting two pictures here, one of the leader standing and another of everyone standing around the meeting room.

"Have the leader stand," Suzanne replied. "But never let anyone get so comfortable they want to drag the meeting on and on."

What a great idea, I thought. I couldn't wait to try it. I stopped taking notes for a moment to ask a question: "On another subject about time-savers — any help with the endless paperwork and e-mails that pile up?"

"That's easy, Taylor. Look for ways to **prioritize and organize**. Time-management books tell you to handle paper only once. When something comes across your desk, either get it filed or take action on it. If it's informational material, put it into a folder marked 'read later.' I use airplane travel time for just that — going through my 'read later' file. Then when it's read, I either toss it, file it when I get home or mark actions I want to take. Again, handle it only once. You'll be amazed how this one little practice helps."

Suzanne kept going. "As for e-mail, I've found that checking it twice a day is enough — once in the morning and once in mid-afternoon. It's a distracting habit to check your e-mail more often than that, unless you're expecting something important from a client or a higher-up.

"Now, what about you? Can you think of anything you're already doing that buys you time?" Suzanne had a knack for getting me to come up with my own ideas and answers.

"Hmmm. Well, one thing that I've learned is to **say 'no' to nonessentials**. No wasn't in my vocabulary until I became a manager. With all I have going on, though, I just can't do everything I'd like to do, and sometimes I say 'no' when I'd much rather take part in an activity or join a community organization. One other rule I follow: I **stay away from office politics**. It's too time-consuming, believe me." I could hear an edge in my voice. "It's much simpler to stay above the muck and mire."

Suzanne remembered one more point to share with me.

"Those are good things to do, Taylor. One more tip I might mention that helps me. Airplane time or any **uninterrupted time is when I do my planning**. If I'm not traveling, I use early morning — before work — to plan my day. I'm freshest early in the morning, so that works for me."

"Well, that's good news! I'm glad our meetings are first thing in the morning," I joked.

I caught a hint of a smile as Suzanne kept her focus and asked, "Okay. So what's first on your to-do list from this morning's ideas, Taylor?"

"The story of the sandbox helped. I'll decide what my big rocks are, sort out and limit the pebbles, sift through the sand, and watch for too much water. I need to be more in control when it comes to managing my time, and that will automatically allow more time for the sand. I'll force myself to focus on what's necessary, not just what's important. If I do all this, I should be able to find time to minimize the amount of water I have to deal with and work smarter, not harder. I'm looking forward to trying all this and sharing these ideas with the team. It should help all of us, Suzanne."

Realizing our time had all but disappeared, we grabbed our empty cups and dropped them in the trash container on the way out. "Thanks for the advice, Suzanne. I've got lots to work on this week. See you at yoga, and I'll report successes next Monday."

"Sounds good! Bye, Taylor. Good luck this week," Suzanne said as she waved and walked to her car.

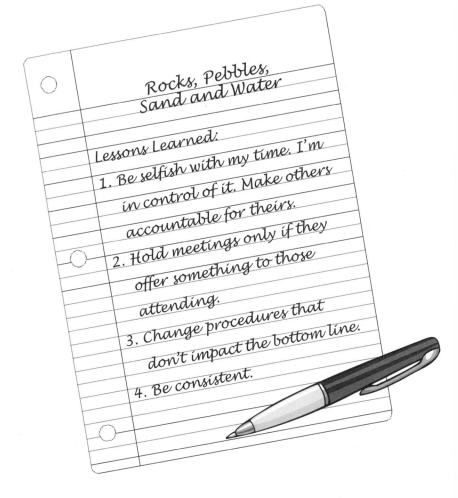

Rocks, Pebbles, Sand and Water

Lessons Learned:

1. Be selfish with my time. I'm in control of it. Make others accountable for theirs.

2. Hold meetings only if they offer something to those attending.

3. Change procedures that don't impact the bottom line.

4. Be consistent.

The Third Monday

The Platinum Rule

*F*or once I was actually up early and had a few minutes to gather my thoughts as I drove to meet Suzanne that next Monday morning.

During the past week, I had had several opportunities to apply what we had discussed last Monday morning. Even at home, I took the advice to simplify and organize. One easy thing I did was to cook twice as much dinner a few nights and freeze half for the next week. Another time-saver was preparing much of the boys' lunches the night before — like mixing up sandwich fillings, putting their veggies and finger foods in plastic baggies, all ready to be put in their backpacks.

I smiled inwardly as I walked in and saw that Suzanne was next in line at the counter. Just as I fell in behind, I heard her order something different — a latte with whip. Hmm, sounded good, and didn't I say I needed to do things differently?

"Make mine the same," I said. Suzanne turned around and grinned as she heard my voice.

"Changing your standard, huh?" she said as we headed to a table. Our comfy corner chairs were already taken. Oh, well. As we sat down at a nearby table, she wanted to know about Josh's soccer game over the weekend.

That's part of why I liked Suzanne so much. She had the ability to make small talk and yet get to the point when she needed to.

"So did you *stick to it* last week? she asked. "I found myself being reminded of watching those boulders in my life getting bigger and bigger." Suzanne was quick to admit those times she needed to practice what she preached. "So tell me about your week."

As I moved aside the newspaper left on our table, I began. "It was a great week to practice what we talked about. Our department had several meetings scheduled, so I let the team in on some of your suggestions and asked them to contribute some of their own. I think they actually liked the idea of approaching meetings with some new guidelines. No one questioned me when I limited our weekly meeting to thirty minutes. Amazingly, we got lots done, and our meeting was ten times more productive.

"One team member said she was so glad we'd become more consistent about meeting times and agendas. She'd been frustrated with the way it was before — having to wait for latecomers and dragging out meetings that could have been handled in less time —

but instead of saying anything, she admitted she was getting frustrated. So changing our meetings worked well." I was glad to report successes to Suzanne.

"Then the time came when I needed to shut my door. Thank goodness I'd already told everyone that if something really important came up, I would shut the door to let them know I couldn't be disturbed. I also mentioned your idea of hanging red ribbons outside their cubes. The next day one of the team members brought in bright red ribbons for everyone. So I think we've started something that will help all of us with interruptions. It was easy, Suzanne. No one balked at all."

"Well, that's what little things can do for us. It's that old 'inch by inch' proverb again. I'm glad you're pleased with the results, but you'll have to take some of the credit for daring to make those changes. So what's the topic for this morning?" Suzanne asked.

I wasn't too well prepared to provide the topic, but I did have a question. "Half my team are new players, and I'm their new boss. With all the work we have to do, it's important we use each other as resources. We all have our strengths, and we should get to know each other better as we work together more. But who's got time to get personal at work?

"On several occasions lately, I've tried to get the team together after work for some social time. We need to bond as a team, and I need to get to know my team, but it just hasn't happened. Maybe there's no chemistry because there are always reasons why some team members can't come. Am I reading something into this that isn't there, or is it that they don't care about each other or me?"

Suzanne approached my question with some questions of her own. "Have you asked the group if this is something they'd like to do? Maybe it's simply that they want to get home to their families, just like you do."

"If that's the case, why wouldn't they just be honest and say that? Seems like an easy thing to do," I replied.

"Easy for you to say, Taylor. But remember, you *are* the boss. And some of them don't know you very well. It takes time to build rapport and learn how to work with a new boss, so maybe they thought if they said they'd rather get home to their families, you'd take it personally.

"Do you remember when you first came to the organization? If your boss had asked you to stay late and socialize, what would you have thought?"

"Actually, you have a point. My first thought would have been, 'What? I work all day, have a family waiting, and my boss wants me to give up my evening to socialize with him. What for?' "

"See, Taylor! You'd have taken it negatively when your boss might have had good intentions of doing just what you're trying to do — getting people to know each other better. But time is a valuable commodity, and most of us work hard *at work*. After work, our time is our own, **not** the organization's time. So how could your team get to know each other and you without spending time after hours? Why don't you give it some thought?"

"Okay, let me think about it some more and come up with Plan B. That shouldn't be too hard," I said. Still, that wasn't the whole point. "But, Suzanne, is this a little thing or not? Can we be a cohesive a team and keep our private lives private? I'm the kind of person who would like to have the team know about my children, my family and what they mean to me. Maybe that's just me."

"What's important here, Taylor, is to realize that we're all individuals — no two alike. Some people are open books, and others are more introverted. That's all. Some people think differently from you and communicate differently. It doesn't make your style right or wrong — just different.

"Here's a good analogy about differences in people. Think about a child's birthday. You and Michael buy a bicycle for one of the boys. It comes in pieces, and you two have to put it together the night before the much-anticipated party. Now, how would you and Michael approach this project differently?" She raised her eyebrows in question.

I paused and smiled because we had done just that project last year, delivering a bright-green bicycle on the morning of Josh's birthday. Michael and I spent several hours the night before putting it together.

"Since this really happened, and not too long ago, I'll tell you exactly what we did. Michael took out the instructions and started reading how to put it together, step-by-step. He started taking one piece at a time out of the box and laying it neatly on the floor. An hour later, I got frustrated, dumped all the parts out at once and then started putting them in what I thought was a logical order. I mean, it's pretty easy to see where the wheels and handles go, isn't it?" I laughed.

"But Michael was adamant about his more methodical way, saying my way would never get the job done right. I thought we'd never get the silly thing together."

Suzanne made the point, "See? You two approached putting it together — and differently — but it *did* get done, didn't it?" She was making a statement, not asking a question.

"So the point I'm making is that the two of you just approached the task of putting the bike together in different ways. Nobody was wrong; both of you were right. That's what happens at work. People think differently, approach their work differently, and the work does get done. Right?"

I agreed.

"So some people are logical and analytical and more introverted. They may want quiet time after work — without socializing. Others are like you, more extroverted and people-oriented, and they love to be with other people. Thank goodness — this is what makes the workplace so rich. It's called 'diversity.' "

"Once again you're making it clear," I admitted. "I haven't taken these differences into consideration. I really thought having everyone over to my home would be appreciated." I frowned at my ignorance.

"Don't worry, Taylor," Suzanne hastened to offer comfort. "It's not a big deal. What *is* a big deal is treating people using what's been called the "Platinum Rule.'"

"I know what the Golden Rule is, but what do you mean by the "Platinum Rule?"

"Let me explain," she continued. "As you know, the Golden Rule tells us to do unto others as we would have them do unto us. The intent is good, but what if you like to be treated with lots of interaction and someone else would just as soon be left alone to get the work done? The Platinum Rule says, *'Do unto others as they would like you to do unto them.'* Simply understand that your way is not always someone else's way when it comes to interacting at work. See the difference?"

Suzanne was right. I had been trying to force the social hour because it was my way of getting this new team to gel. I hadn't imagined that others on the team wouldn't want to do the same. I was taking copious notes on our conversation when another point hit me.

"I guess I need to **put myself in someone else's shoes**. Is that what you're saying, Suzanne?"

"That's exactly what I'm saying. Too often, managers try to manage everyone the same. And it doesn't work. Management has never been a one-size-fits-all discipline. In fact, have you ever heard someone say, 'Well, I'm just the way I am, and you can take me or leave me'? I'm afraid that attitude will keep that person from being successful at building relationships. Leaders, on the other hand, are great at discerning differences and building relationships. Therein lies the difference between leaders and bosses.

"Have you ever known bosses who manage with a 'my way or the highway' attitude? These rigid people are doomed to fail eventually because in today's workplace, flexibility is a key to success. Some call it 'agility' — being able to make room for any and every personality in whatever scenario that's playing. If you're not agile or flexible, people won't perform. It's as simple as that." Suzanne waited for my response.

"Although I haven't thought about it in exactly those terms," I said, "I *do* have a diverse team. Some have been around longer than I've been working. They probably have been cringing when I've tried to force meetings after work, and it probably did look like my way or else. I can see that now, Suzanne. What a mistake that was! But let me try some things this week, and I'll let you know next Monday what happens."

"Well, give it a try. Let's get to work. I've got a busy day, and I don't want you to be late. One important attribute of a leader, Taylor, is timeliness. See you at yoga."

"Right, Suzanne. Thanks. Have a great week."

I was determined I'd view my team through a different set of lenses — looking at each person individually and recognizing what made them unique.

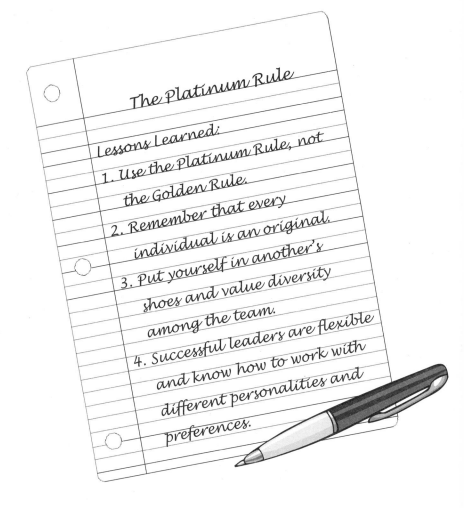

The Platinum Rule

Lessons Learned:

1. Use the Platinum Rule, not the Golden Rule.

2. Remember that every individual is an original.

3. Put yourself in another's shoes and value diversity among the team.

4. Successful leaders are flexible and know how to work with different personalities and preferences.

The Fourth Monday

Managing Sideways

*T*his Monday morning was going to be hard for me. A situation had come up with Brandon, a peer in another department, and I had really blown it.

Suzanne and I had talked just last week about putting myself in someone else's shoes, but I still blew it. The truth I have come to realize is that I apparently don't have much patience with people who don't react as quickly as I'd like. My tendency is to just do it myself.

I arrived promptly, wanting Suzanne to know I had heard her last week when she said, "Timeliness is an attribute of a successful leader." As we moved to a table near the front of the shop, I got right to the point.

"Suzanne, I know there's value in different styles, like we discussed last week. But when people don't complete assignments on time or when they give me information that isn't usable, I get frustrated. Last week I lost my temper when I asked Brandon, my peer in another department, to give me a report on the status of a new project. He took forever to get the report to me, and when he did, it had more graphs and charts than someone on an expedition would need.

"I have a real problem when it comes to managing sideways with people who don't report to me."

Suzanne seemed to understand my point right away. "What a great term — managing sideways — and you're right! Working with other departments *is* trying to manage sideways.

"Not that it will improve your situation, but you're not alone in this. As companies have downsized, people's scope of reach has increased. The challenge is to work effectively with people we rely on as resources to deliver what we need to do our jobs effectively, and when we have no authority over these people, it can definitely be difficult.

"But let me ask you a question. Just what is your scope of reach? What other departments do you rely on for information, reports or other support that you need to do your job?"

"Well, I regularly have to work with the finance department, operations, marketing, human resources and collections. Some of them work really well with me and are responsive whenever I have a request, but Brandon is always late and really doesn't seem to care about my department or me!

"How can I get him to understand I wouldn't ask if I didn't need something? It's not like I'm asking for busy work!" I could hear my voice getting louder. I knew my frustration was showing.

"You're going to have to build a relationship with Brandon, Taylor. You need to find ways to influence, rather than command, when you have no control. Did you clash with Brandon because he didn't value your request or because it was a result of Brandon doing things for his reasons, not yours?" she asked.

"I hadn't thought of it that way. I guess most of us do things for our own reasons," I admitted.

"It's all about relationships, Taylor," Suzanne began, "and it's about working collaboratively toward a clear goal. You're both trying to accomplish a result that meets the organization's larger goal. Right? The trick is to agree on what that the common goal is and what part each of you will play in achieving it."

Suzanne's answer hit the nail on the head, as usual, but she wasn't ready to end the meeting.

"Most organizations operate under the 95/5 Rule, Taylor. That rule tells us that workgroups understand 95 percent of what goes on within their own team. Of course, a small number of things happen that may be a mystery, but most of the time the team knows the majority of what goes on within their group.

"The 5 percent is what the team knows about other departments.

Of course, it would be unreasonable to expect anyone to know 100 percent about what's going on within other workgroups, but is it logical to know so little about how the big picture comes together?" Suzanne paused to take a sip of coffee.

"If you can tear down the walls and understand more of what's going on in other areas of your organization, it will destroy misconceptions of other departments, and teams can begin supporting each other.

"So if you were in Brandon's shoes, what do you think might have been going on in his department that kept him from responding quickly?" she asked.

"I don't have a clue. And that's not my concern, is it?" I asked defensively. "I have to get my report in, but I can't complete it without his information." My voice was rising again.

Suzanne shrugged. "Let's look at managing sideways with Brandon, and maybe we can come up with a plan to try when you're working on your next report. One thing for sure — we all do better when we have clear expectations of each other.

"So how about this? First, do you know what Brandon's priorities are? And does he know what yours are and why you're asking for information by a certain date?"

"Hmm. I guess I assumed if I asked for information by a certain date, he'd know I needed it by that date — no reason to explain.

Or is there?" I asked. I was beginning to see where she was going. "So it would help to first ask Brandon *whether* he would be able to get me the information by a certain time and then explain why I had that deadline. Right?"

"Absolutely, Taylor," she agreed. "Most important, though, if Brandon understands that helping you get that report in on time means the entire division benefits, then he can see how it's in his best interest to help the cause. You see, what you're doing is getting him in the boat with you so you can both paddle in the same direction. Both departments benefit when your projections are made on time.

"The hard reality is, **people do things for their reasons, not yours.** Remember?"

"So let's see if I can put this managing sideways thing in perspective," I said as I thought through the process. "First, I can't demand. I can only influence. You know, Suzanne, I think influencing is something that's a natural inclination for most women. So I need to capitalize on that," I answered confidently.

"That's a good point, and I couldn't agree more," she added with a smile. "Influencing is the best way to get others to do something while maintaining a positive relationship. Not only that, but effective influencing gives you an edge toward achieving your goals faster."

"I can see how important that type of influencing can be in the workplace," I agreed. "What's worked for you? You seem to be a pro at this." I wanted all the **how-to**'s on the subject.

"It seems to me, Taylor, that this is — once again — putting yourself in someone else's shoes. Here's what works for me:

1. Have a clear goal and know specifically what I need to have the other person do before starting a conversation.

2. During our conversation, I consider what's going on within the other person's organization. I always check my assumptions by asking. Maybe my peer is on his own deadline. Maybe he just returned from a business trip and has a lot to catch up on. You never know. So I try to think about the other person's perspective.

3. Once I know the situation, I work toward getting a shared commitment that includes specific time lines. Maybe this sounds complicated, but the time I take thinking through these steps seems to help avoid clashes and confrontations at the other end."

It did seem time-consuming, but I figured if Suzanne took the time, so should I.

"No, actually it makes sense, Suzanne. I'm usually in such a rush. It's more of a one-way conversation, usually all my way. As you've said many times, it's the relationship that counts."

Suzanne continued, "You asked me once — before we started

our meetings — the reasons why our firm is such a great place to work. One reason is that David, our CEO, has shifted everyone's perspective when it comes to working together.

"Today's environment calls for a new mind-set. We all need to be shifting our thinking on how we must work across the organization — from west to east — rather than from the top down. More often than not, we *are* managing sideways.

"David knew the old management behavior of command and control — command your employees every step of the way and control their every move — wouldn't cut it. Our managers now see their role as being more responsible, horizontally and system-wide.

"What that means is we pay close attention to working successfully across departments and nurturing those relationships. **People respond positively to people they know, trust and like.** We're all committed to embracing the whole picture and how our part aligns with our clients. David calls it being 'client-centric'— thinking about how each department serves the client. If we think in these terms, then everyone wants to work together. This type of culture encourages win-win relationships at every level."

I was seeing new horizons for the first time — understanding and agreeing with everything I saw.

Suzanne continued. "Your job as a manager is not only to pay attention to what your team does, but also to think about the whole process and how it connects with the customer. So you must **hold yourself and your team individually accountable for all cross-functional consequences.**

"Taylor, there's no longer room for people to have personal agendas focused on their own performance at the expense of the whole. Everyone needs to align with the company's common goal." Suzanne was clear and passionate as she made each point, leaning across the table for emphasis as she outlined three suggestions:

"First, **be certain everyone understands the big picture.** How do you create value for the customer? Common sense would say that since customers probably interact with lots of departments, your team must interact with other teams across departments to get the job done. If there's a glitch, it needs to be handled quickly so that, from the customer's viewpoint, their service is seamless.

"Second, once the big picture is in place, you don't have time, Taylor, to make all the decisions. As manager, your job is to **have a broad grasp of the business** and to know how each step of the work gets done. Then you must depend on your team to know the details…so you have to teach them the business of the business. Let them be self-sufficient to get their various jobs accomplished.

"Third, **communicate to the max!** Use a variety of ways to keep communication flowing. Use notes, conversations, e-mails and Post-Its to encourage this flow of information. Stay accessible. Encourage two-way communication and be a careful listener. With so many people handling bits and pieces of a process, communication is key."

"As usual, every word makes sense." I admitted. "I definitely hear what you're saying — that I not only have to manage my team, but to help them manage sideways with their peers, just like I have to manage sideways with mine. It's almost too simple, but it certainly makes sense, Suzanne."

This brought up another question I had on my mind. "Since we're talking about managing others, how should I manage my boss? That's a concept that's eluded me since day one," I said.

"Well, Taylor, it starts with putting yourself in someone else's shoes again. Just like you're doing with Brandon, what about anticipating your boss and his needs, then trying to help him get what he wants? Think about this scenario: You're the boss of your team. What happens when a team member doesn't complete a task?"

"Oooh, that's a no-no. I not only would get angry, but I also would tend to question that person's accountability," I fired back.

"Okay, so you send the person back to get it completed, or you do it yourself. Right?" she asked.

"Exactly!"

"Now, wouldn't it be great if that person thought about what *you* are focused on and what *your* challenges are and then completed their tasks that not only met your needs, but also maybe even solved a problem two levels up from you?" Suzanne suggested.

"I would be elated," I said, "and for that kind of performance, that person would rate a place at the top of my promotion list," I said. "Now, let me see if I understand how to handle *my* boss, using your suggestions:

- Anticipate the boss's needs and help the boss get what he or she wants and needs.

- Solve problems that would satisfy two levels up from me.

- Know my boss's focus.

- Know the challenges confronting the boss, then complete tasks that require only the boss's concurrence or sign-off."

"You've got it," Suzanne said, glancing at her watch. "Whew, we've covered a lot of ground in one hour this morning, but what we've talked about does make a difference in your effectiveness as a manager.

"All of the issues and suggestions we've discussed have helped our firm become a great place to work. So think about your role this week on three levels — managing downward with your team, managing sideways with your peers and managing up with your boss — accomplishing each by using your influencing skills. You can do this, Taylor." She squeezed my arm as we left the table.

"Now let's get going. You've got plenty on your plate for this week. Try a little at a time, and I'll see you at yoga."

As I walked out of Starbucks, I felt energized. Suzanne had made me see my role as I had never seen it before. I knew there was an art to mastering all three types of management — downward, sideways and upward — but I had a lot to digest, and I wanted to give it a try, taking it one step at a time.

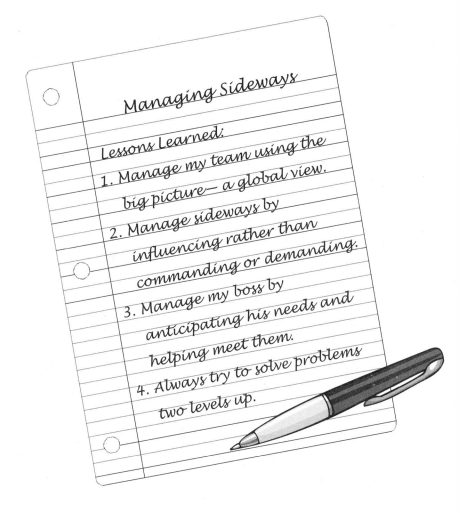

Managing Sideways

Lessons Learned:

1. Manage my team using the big picture— a global view.

2. Manage sideways by influencing rather than commanding or demanding.

3. Manage my boss by anticipating his needs and helping meet them.

4. Always try to solve problems two levels up.

The Fifth Monday

Living In Raplexity

E ntering Starbucks early the next Monday morning, I was amazed at how many people were in line. The place was packed, so I got my coffee and grabbed a table outside to enjoy the bright crisp morning. "Amazing," I thought. "Starbucks has become such a phenomenon."

There was no sign of Suzanne. As I read the morning's headlines, she appeared across the table, perfectly groomed and dressed to perfection, as usual.

"Sorry, you beat me to it this morning, Taylor." She put her things down and joined the order line. As she walked back to our table, I was thinking how much help she had given me these few weeks. It was energizing to consider the possibilities that I could someday do the same for others. Experience certainly is the best teacher.

"So, Taylor," she began, " last week you had lots to think about.

How did you do with Brandon?"

"You know, your advice last week really did help!" I proudly stated. "I found out that Brandon's department was going through its own issues. His boss was promoted, and his workgroup was waiting to hear who the new boss would be. All they knew was it would be someone from the outside.

"I know Brandon is not the type who deals well with ambiguity. He's a pretty black-and-white kind of guy. So the challenge of change had him reeling. Not that that's an excuse, but at least he opened up to me. When I explained my need for timeliness on that report, he was quick to apologize and said next time he would be on time. So I think our candid conversation helped our relationship for the future, just like you said.

"Speaking of ambiguity and change, you'll never believe what else I was faced with this week. We're merging with another firm — a competitor! Can you believe it? Just when I'm making progress. Now I'm not even sure if I'll have a job! The rumor mill is running at warp speed, and of course I don't have any answers for my team — or myself.

"My people expect me to know what's going on. I feel so out of control because I don't know any more than they do, and to make matters worse, we were told it would be a while before there would be more information.

"Can you believe our senior management wants to wait until

things are tightened down before letting the rest of us know anything? How can they think we can do our work when we're not being given any answers?" I caught my breath, forcing myself to slow down.

I felt like a fire hose, spewing out words faster than Suzanne could take them in. To my surprise, she stayed calm.

"That's a reality of business today," Suzanne began. She didn't seem surprised at all.

"We're living in a world of **raplexity**, Taylor. I heard that word from a management guru in a seminar recently. It means *living in a business environment that changes rapidly, and, as changes occur, they are more and more complex.* So put those two elements together and you get raplexity. I like that word, don't you?"

I let this first bit of information sink in.

"I went through some frustration like this last year when our firm went through a merger," Suzanne continued. "So often, mergers and acquisitions cause people worry, even to the point of losing productivity.

"Check out the facts. Out of 10,000 or so merger or acquisition transactions in the United States every year, 75 percent fail to meet the pre-merger expectations. It's not just your organization, either," she said, reassuringly. "What I've come to realize is that most businesses are constantly going through changes — some small, some significant. If it's not a merger or acquisition, it's reorganization, relocation, downsizing, upsizing — it seems companies don't even know what size is the right size anymore."

She smiled slightly. I felt she was making light of the facts, while I was truly worried — about my job, my department and my team. I'd probably get a new boss or maybe even be without a job, just when I was beginning to make progress with my team and with Doug, my boss. During the time I had reported to him this year, we'd managed to maintain a good relationship, at least most of the time.

As for Suzanne's comments about constant change, I said, "That's all well and good, but I'm the manager, and I think I should have more information to tell my employees so they don't get all stressed out."

"Actually, Taylor, that's a burden you can release. You can tell them only what you know. **There's nothing wrong with honestly saying, 'I don't know.'** Just be careful *not* to add the words '*but I'll find out*'. That's what we all want to say, isn't it?"

"Absolutely! Isn't that my job — to find out and report back to my team?" I asked.

"Not exactly," Suzanne answered. "Think about this. If your boss said, 'I don't know, but I'll find out,' what would you think?"

"Well, I guess that would say to me there *is* an answer and he'll come back with it," I said.

"Okay, and what would you do until you got his answer?" she continued to probe.

"Honestly, I'd probably be distracted until he came back with the answer, so my productivity wouldn't be great. I sure wouldn't work on something that might be changed. So I'd work only on those things I was sure would matter," I answered.

"Taylor, now that you're a manager, you know there may *not* be answers for every question you're asked. There will also be some cases when the answer may not be known, so honesty is always the best policy. The honest answer when you don't know *is*, 'I don't know.'

"But commit to your team that as soon as *you* know something, they'll know. How about this? When someone asks you for an answer you don't have, say something like, 'I don't know, but what could we focus on in the meantime until we get more answers?' "

Suzanne made a good point. I couldn't possibly have all the answers for my team, especially with all the rumors whirling around us, and we can't afford to waste energy on the unknowns.

"That's a great comeback," I said. "It takes me off the hook when team members come to me for answers and I really don't have them. It makes them accountable for continuing to get the work done. What a good idea! I'm sure I'll have plenty of opportunities to try that out this week," I said.

"And you're doing something else that a good manager should do, Taylor," Suzanne added. "You're helping people **focus on things that are in their control**. Think about it. How do any of us feel when we don't have control?"

"I hate that feeling."

"Sure," she continued. "As professionals, we like to feel we have control over our lives, our destiny and our work. So in essence you're giving them something they *can* control and feel good about at the same time, even during a period of not knowing.

"That in turn will sustain productivity. I believe most people want to be productive, don't you?" Suzanne asked rhetorically. "During times of change, however, they aren't sure what to focus on first. You need to keep your team from getting too disoriented in these blurry times when none of you can see the big picture clearly."

I added, "Now, I *am* smart enough to know that change is just part of an organization's growth process. I just want to be sure my team's morale doesn't drop through the floor, so I need to know what to expect, Suzanne.

"Since you successfully guided your organization through the merger last year, what did you experience?"

I was taking copious notes as I did every Monday morning.

"I recognized, as a leader," she said soberly, "that our management team was accountable not only for helping ourselves but also to our employees and the entire firm as we successfully implemented the changes as quickly as possible. We spent exhaustive energy to clearly understand how a merger would affect us.

"During that time we realized that our need to merge was really driven by a need to position ourselves in the marketplace, and in order to remain competitive, we had to grow. So marketplace demands were really driving those changes we were making — and don't you think the same holds true in your company's situation, Taylor?"

"I guess so," I agreed hesitantly, "but what can I do to make this easier for our team?"

Suzanne was ready with an answer. "Well, you might think about positioning your changes positively. In our company, we were committed to looking at our merger not with a sense of loss, but rather as a growth opportunity, just as you said earlier. The hard part, of course, was to educate the employees so they would put aside their expectations that change would go away. Once this education took hold, changes came more quickly, and everyone was made accountable for making this merger successful.

"We certainly found that it wasn't easy for people to see all this. And it's not going to be easy for your team, either. They'll get wound up in their own *me* issues, so expect that."

Suzanne took a breath and then continued. "It was evident from the beginning of the merger activity that **communication was vital**.

Employees want to hear messages about change from two people: the CEO or their immediate supervisor — and these messages are not the same. So I set in place all kinds of methods to communicate across the organization.

"We kept people informed. David, our CEO, held monthly videoconferences to give updates. All department leaders held their own meetings to let people ask questions. Those meetings gave us a chance to **get resistance out in the open and to deal with it**. We knew that the top obstacle to successful change is employee resistance at all levels. And we also knew that there are three reasons for employee resistance — lack of awareness about the change, comfort with the ways things are and fear of the unknown.

"We didn't hesitate to give answers when we had them, but we were also honest about telling people we didn't know when we didn't. That constant communication was two-way, and it made a huge difference in people's trust and comfort levels.

"Look at it this way, Taylor. What do you think people would've done if we had *not* communicated regularly?"

I knew that was a leading question!

"They'd probably make up their own answers, and there'd be a galaxy of rumors spreading," I finally answered. "That's exactly what's happening in my company."

Now I saw the dilemma.

"You're absolutely right," Suzanne said. "So you can see why constant communication is a must.

"The next thing we did successfully was **focus on productivity**. There's a definite productivity curve that happens during times of change. It looks like this," she said, sketching the curve on a piece of paper she had slipped out of her planner.

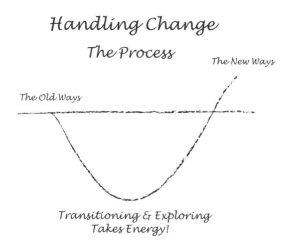

Handling Change
The Process

The New Ways

The Old Ways

Transitioning & Exploring
Takes Energy!

Her drawing helped me visualize what she explained next.

"Taylor, think about the first day on your new job," Suzanne said. "You went from being an individual contributor to a manager. Was it an easy transition to let go of the place where you were comfortable and successful? And once you started your new duties, did you have a period of time when you actually lost productivity as you were learning your new role?"

"Very definitely," I remembered. "I can see clearly how this picture fits. In fact, I still feel I'm in transition. But why is this picture showing a dip? I don't think I dropped the ball along the way!" I said.

"I'm sure you didn't," she continued. "But wouldn't you also agree that you experienced a bit of an energy drain as you took on new and different responsibilities?"

"That's true," I said.

"Well, then, you can see how people have a hard time letting go of the old ways, old cultures and old practices as change forces them to transition into a new environment and new ways of doing business. During our company's transition, the trick for us was to get people to say goodbye to their old ways.

"Our next challenge was to help people navigate through a transition phase that was filled with confusion and frustration. We knew that those feelings were naturally associated with a merger or any major change, and we wanted to develop a smooth transition from what **was** to what **would be** at our firm."

Suzanne explained that during any time of transitioning, it is difficult because nothing is on autopilot and everything takes more thought, time and energy. She also pointed out that middle managers often resist change during transitions because of fear of losing control as well as being overloaded with responsibilities.

Then came a warning: "So be careful, Taylor. Your attitude matters right now. Your team is going to be watching for your reactions and taking their cues from you about how to proceed."

She continued: "Finally, we helped people embrace the new ways, systems and procedures, and we showed them how to take advantage of new opportunities. We did this in six months, which is about the norm for a successful transition, and that short timeframe helped make it a relatively smooth transition where productivity didn't have a chance to drop for long."

"What are you showing with the curved line going above the bar at the words new ways?" I asked.

"That simply means if it was necessary to make the change in the first place, then productivity should actually be better after the merger than before. Now, I know what you're going to ask, Taylor. How did we do this?

"First, we got people to **focus on critical priorities**. Productivity had to be protected. And we knew it was important to *do the right things* rather than hammer on *doing things exactly right*."

"Suzanne, are you giving me a short version of an MBA here?" I chuckled. But it did seem overwhelming. "Please go on. It's great stuff," I urged, continuing to take notes as quickly as I could.

"As we went through the reorganization and integrated new processes, managers had to give more hands-on guidance and direction. We framed out specific roles and responsibilities, leaving no room for vagueness. People **focused on their 'main things,'** those things that were important to the business and our customers.

"Remember those big rocks we put in the jar first? When changes occurred at our company, we set targeted goals — big rocks, so to speak — so each team knew their main thing. If someone from a different department asked one of our people to do something that was not their main thing, our managers supported them in saying no. This not only worked, but it made people feel they were a part of the *firm's* main thing, not just their own.

"We asked our teams to **focus intensely on short-term objectives.** Long-term goal setting takes more time and effort, and there's more guesswork involved. We wanted people to gain confidence from seeing the short-term goals achieved — and they did. We watched our employees get pumped up and energized.

"When short-term objectives were met, we celebrated successes in little ways — like bringing in lunch one day, offering chair massages several times a month and even giving out T-shirts that read, **"Keep the main thing the main thing."**

I took my last sip of coffee. "This is really a good explanation of what I can expect with our merger. I'm glad to have your thoughts, Suzanne. So in a time of change, do you think everyone will get on board? I'm hearing lots of rumors and watching people become resistant. Some people just don't like to have their world turned topsy-turvy, and that's how this merger is being viewed. Me included, I must add."

"Taylor, as the manager you must put on your happy face, even when you don't feel like it. It's tough enough dealing with the uncertainties and fears your team may be experiencing. People are watching you to see your reaction.

"Just remember that this merger was done for good business reasons, some you may not be privy to. Even so, management's role is to make the changes work, period!" She was firm on this.

"I can do that," I smiled. "I'm a pretty optimistic person, as you know."

"Yes, you are. And to remain optimistic, be aware of where you're spending your time and with whom. Look at this."

20% - Champions
50% - Fence sitters
30% - Resisters

"Experts have studied the idea that people fall into three categories based on the way they approach change. **Twenty percent** will get behind it and champion the cause. They'll be your supporters, putting their energy into actions that move the ball forward. They'll look beyond themselves and commit to the outcome the organization is trying to achieve. They could actually get excited about this merger, seeing all kinds of opportunities for themselves.

"**Fifty percent** will be fence-sitters. These are the ones who will wait for direction without proactively taking charge of their own careers. They haven't decided which side to move toward, so you'll see them stalling and waiting for more information before they get too involved. When a decision is made, they'll move cautiously and will keep looking back and questioning. They'll spend their energy figuring out what all this means to them personally.

"**Thirty percent** will become defiant and will resist changes or whatever else is going on. They'll push back or even try to sabotage the process. They'll waste energy on spreading false information or even starting a rumor mill.

"Now, Taylor, as a manager of these three groups, where do you think you should spend your time?" she asked pointedly.

I thought I had the right answer. "Probably with the last 30 percent, so they don't cause too much confusion to the rest of the team. I should try to motivate them, I think."

"Many managers would answer the same." Suzanne persisted, saying, "Let me ask you this. When was the last time you tried to motivate someone like these 30 percenters, and what results did you get?"

She was coaching me to see the situation realistically. I had to take off my rose-colored glasses and look at the hard reality.

"Now that you mention it, I think a woman I tried to work with last month was a 30 percenter." I said. "Jill has been around a long time, and I was making a change in procedure that involved her role. She fought me all the way, trying to convince me that she could continue doing her work the same way and it wouldn't make any difference. To your point, there was nothing I could do to convince her to try a better way, even when I showed her it was an easier way to accomplish her job," I admitted.

"And how much time did you spend trying to motivate and convince her, Taylor?" Suzanne asked.

"Obviously, too much! I see your point. So are you saying to spend my time with the 20 percenters?"

Suzanne clarified by saying, "Not exactly. Look at the 50 percenters as recruits. They're waiting to be recruited, either up or down. Your job is to try to get more people in the middle to become change agents you can rely on. Get them involved and reward their positive behaviors. Spend your time above the last line, and you'll keep your own energy up, knowing these are the folks you can count on to do the hard work!

"Don't waste time and energy with 30 percenters when it's their choice to be either a positive or negative influence. They'll see they aren't getting any attention and do one of two things: either get themselves fired or quit the business, which is their choice. So re-recruit your winners, Taylor. You need them."

"One more thing, Suzanne, and then I know our time is up. Didn't you personally get stressed when your organization went through the merger, even though it was successful?"

"Sure," Suzanne said. "All I could do was recognize where I had control over my stress. I found ways to align my team with those decisions being made for business reasons. Whether I agreed or not, it would only cause stress to fight the changes. I knew I'd be much better off to look at *why*, from a business perspective, these changes were being made. Then I did everything I could to side with those changes. Only then could I see the possibilities that could lie ahead."

She paused while she began gathering up her materials to leave. "Does all this make sense, or are you more confused than when we started this morning?" Suzanne asked simply.

I took a deep breath. "Well, to tell you the truth, this won't be easy for any of us, but you certainly have given me good tools to see and do things differently, that's for sure."

As we walked toward the door, she kept talking. "Taylor, I want you to know it's great for me to spend time with you each week because it reinforces good management strategies for me as I share them with you. That said, tell me what you're going to do this week."

"There's so much to do, I'm not sure where to start," I responded. "I think I'll start by watching where I spend my time and energy. I'll also be very aware of where people are emotionally so I can be a better listener and help them move forward. Believe me, I've got my work cut out for me, but I'm up to it. Thanks so much for this advice, and have a good week, yourself, Suzanne!"

I left hurriedly to get to another meeting, feeling somewhat relieved by knowing I had found tools to handle this challenge.

Living In Raplexity

Lessons Learned:
1. It's ok to say, "I don't know."
2. Know the main thing and do the main thing.
3. Communication is crucial during times of change.
4. Hold people accountable for their tasks at hand.

The Sixth Monday

Hire Tough

*I*t was hard to get out of bed that next Monday morning. How I wanted to curl up and stay cozy on this drizzly, rainy day! The kids had been cooped up all weekend, and Michael and I had spent time inside with them doing crafts, baking cookies and reading some new books. Grade school age is great, and we had fun!

As I left to meet Suzanne, I took a few minutes to reflect on how blessed I felt to have my sweet family. Like anything else, it took effort to keep family time separate from work time and to carve out portions of the week where we could enjoy time together. It's that "balance thing" we all talk about, I mused, wondering if I'd ever master it.

"Hey there, Taylor," I heard Suzanne's voice coming from the parking lot. "Wait up."

As we walked into Starbucks together, she mentioned she was

scheduled on a flight to New York immediately after our meeting. I knew she always had a busy schedule, yet here she was taking time with me. It was wonderful to have someone committed to being my mentor. I vowed I would be just as committed when the opportunity came for me to mentor another individual.

"You're so kind to take this time, Suzanne," I said again. "I'm sure you could've used this extra hour to pack and get ready."

"Not a problem. This is important to both of us, Taylor. I pride myself in holding up my end of the bargain, just as you've done. But I *have* to leave right on the hour.

"So what's up? How's the merger going? And how's your team?" she asked.

After getting our coffee, I hit the issue head on. "It was amazing to watch people through a different set of lenses last week. I especially noticed those 30 percenters and their behaviors.

"Do you remember Jill, the woman I mentioned? She was the one who refused to move to a different process for doing her work, even when I showed her it was easier. Well, she quit this week. I guess she just didn't want to bother with going through the merger and having to make more changes."

"How do you feel about that?" Suzanne asked.

"I think her resignation was for the best, and I'll find a replacement, I'm sure. In fact, I'm looking for two at the moment. Another man took the early retirement package that was offered. He's a nice guy, but I must say he didn't give his job his all, if you know what I mean."

"Yes, I think I do. Sounds like now you have a chance to make good hires and add to the team. So what are your plans?"

"Actually, I've just started the search. Our human resources department is looking internally, and I've started the outside search through an agency we regularly use. Any advice on what to look for? I need to hurry and get this done, but I don't want to make any bad choices," I said.

"You're right. Now's the time to be sure you're hiring more of the 20 percenters we talked about last week. The question is, how can you recognize them among the candidates you interview?"

"Suzanne, I really need a strong team to take us through this tenuous time. If our team doesn't rise to the occasion, competition will bear down harder. I have a chance to change the make-up of my team for the better, and that's what I want to do. Even our ideas are getting stale within the group. Just like a battery, we need to be recharged from time to time, and I think new people might help."

"No doubt. Putting the right people in the right jobs will benefit the entire team. I've always believed in the management principle of **hire tough and manage easy**. What that means is that it takes more time to find the right people," Suzanne agreed.

"So how many people have you hired since you became a manager?" she asked.

"Only one," I said lamely, "but he transferred from another department, and I was told I needed to bring him on board. So I can't say I had much influence in that one. If I had, I'm not sure I would've selected him. He tends to be a slacker, but for now I'm stuck with him. So you might say this is really the first time I'll be hiring on my own."

"Well, I can think of a few pointers to share," Suzanne responded brightly. "Start with recognizing that interviewing skills may not be your strong suit. After all, you don't interview regularly, so rely on your human resources department to give you a process to use. It's sure easier to use what's proven to work instead of trying to reinvent the wheel."

I agreed. This was going to be such an important part of my job. "Okay, let me ask you this. I'm sure HR will help, but I want the final say in picking my people. Yet while I feel like I'm a good judge of character, how can I be sure? Other than the basic questions and reviewing the candidate's resume, what should I look for?"

"One thing you might keep in mind is that **people tend to hire and promote in their own image**," she said. "Let me ask you — have you ever noticed that you usually gravitate toward people who are somewhat like you? As an example, since you have a family, you probably socialize with other families. When you were in school and played sports, you probably enjoyed being around other sports-minded kids. Remember the old saying, 'Birds of a feather flock together'? Do you agree?" Suzanne asked.

"Yes, but are you saying I should find people just like me?" I wasn't sure I understood.

"Actually," she continued after biting into the crumb cake she had ordered, "it's better to staff to your weaknesses so you can focus on your areas of strength. Others who are strong where you are not can fill in the gaps.

"I'm just saying it's critical for you to recognize that people who are different won't be naturally attracted to you and vice versa. You'll be drawn to those like yourself."

She sipped her coffee and kept talking. "The important part of hiring is to **find people like you in key areas such as values, attitudes and leadership ability.** What about the person you mentioned, Taylor? The one you inherited. Does he share your values, attitudes or leadership ability?"

"Absolutely not!" I replied firmly. "He sees a glass half empty, and the rest of the team gets tired of his pessimistic attitude. That sure doesn't make me think of him as having leadership ability. I don't know many leaders who have that kind of half-empty attitude," I said.

"Neither do I. You can't create positive change with a negative attitude." Suzanne was making a good point. She gave me some things to think about.

She also talked a lot about how she is always on the lookout for good people, and that she has a clear view about what kind of people she wants on her team. She went on to say that after I have hired the best people, I should look for those who could take my position. It sounded strange at first. Why would I work myself out of my job? But what she meant was that I should mentor people and look for a successor. What Suzanne gave me that morning was a framework for hiring strong people to create a strong team.

"Okay, that makes perfect sense — hire talented people to create a strong team," I replied, "but how can I interview to make sure I have the strongest candidates when it comes time to make a job offer?"

"The first thing is to **be totally prepared so that you can be a good listener**," Suzanne began. "Someone who is a valuable asset wants to feel that you're investing time to have an effective interview. I can guarantee you that the interviewee knows what to look for, too, Taylor. Here's where human resources can help again. But before you start the interview process and your search for strong team members, be sure you know the rules regarding legal and illegal questions to ask."

She cleared her voice and continued. "Next, you have to know what you're looking for in terms of personality fit with the team.

It's important to have a diverse team with differing ideas and work styles so you can truly leverage their strengths. Just be sure they share common ground in their character and values.

"And don't be afraid to hire people who are better in some areas than you! Yes, I know it sounds threatening, but it's actually a benefit. Hire the best and you'll become the best. Good people make *you* look good."

I felt confident about everything she had said so far. I certainly wasn't afraid or threatened by good people.

"As far as knowing you're making the right choice," Suzanne continued, "I always get others to interview the top candidates. In fact, it's a good idea to have three people interview them and compare opinions.

"For the initial interview, however, it's up to you to look at three areas of need, Taylor — competencies, attitudes and disciplines. Competencies are strengths, such as being a good communicator or negotiator and having the ability to make good presentations, sell ideas effectively or use certain computer software. **Attitude is how they feel about working with others.** Disciplines are the day-to-day activities and behaviors that drive the business.

"Be clear on the competencies you need in a particular role, knowing you can train in additional skills where they're needed. Then also look at how disciplined the person is in getting the daily work done. As the manager, you coach competencies, you offer training for skills needed, and you must manage disciplines. Don't overlook the attitude part. I think that you should hire attitude first because then you can teach skills and discipline. Does this make sense? "

"Actually, yes," I said. "I hadn't thought about these three areas in the same terms you've used. Now that you've explained the various categories to look for in each candidate, I realize how much time I've spent — and probably wasted — with the man I inherited on my team. I know he's competent in his job and has the skills to complete tasks. It's the disciplines I've had to work on with him. He continues to be late to meetings and in getting work done. I've even suggested he enroll in a time-management course, but so far he hasn't followed through," I reflected. "He lacks disciplines and attitude — and those turn out to be the most important for our team."

As I noticed Suzanne looking at her watch, I remembered she had a plane to catch.

"Oops — you'd better go or you'll be late," I said as I started to get up.

"Sorry to have to rush this morning, but the plane won't wait. Good luck this week. It's important to get on this hiring process right away. You'll need a complete team to accomplish all that will be coming your way with merger activities. Gotta run. See you at yoga when I get back."

We both rushed to our cars to start our busy week.

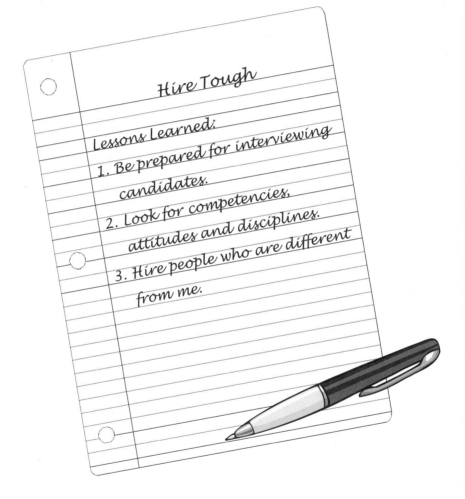

Hire Tough

Lessons Learned:

1. Be prepared for interviewing candidates.

2. Look for competencies, attitudes and disciplines.

3. Hire people who are different from me.

The Seventh Monday

Balancing On Life's High Wire

What an interesting week of interviews! I was amazed at the talent pool and the number of people looking for new careers. Arriving early this Monday morning to go over a few résumés, I secured our corner chairs and began reading.

"Good morning, Suzanne," I said as I looked up to see her coming toward me.

We spent a few minutes talking about her trip to New York and my weekend with the family. She told me she had attended a board meeting, which I didn't even know was on her plate. I marveled at how many activities she seemed so able to juggle.

My job and family were all consuming. I wondered whether I would ever be as organized as she seemed to be. Or did that come with experience? That was a question I wasn't sure was appropriate to ask. Besides, I had other things on my mind that were current challenges I had to confront.

"There are so many good people going through 're-careering,' Suzanne. That's the term I heard mentioned on several occasions this week, meaning changing a career path. Have you heard this?"

"I've heard that word bandied about recently," Suzanne said.

"One of the men I want to hire said he had been working in one industry for his entire 15 years in business. Now, after being laid off, he decided to get a fresh start and re-career his future business opportunities. I think he'd be a great fit for the team, and he really wants to come to work for us," I said.

"Did you find other good candidates last week?" she asked.

"Yes, and that's the good news. In fact, I'll make offers to two of them today. What a relief. The only bad news is that I've been informed the schedules are going to get ratcheted up, which will probably result in more overtime. I'm not afraid of hard work, and I think my prioritizing is helping, but I'm concerned that between late hours at the office and early meetings coming up, Michael and the boys will suffer. How in the world were you able to be so successful in business while raising your son alone and have him turn out to be such a great guy?"

A serious look came upon her as she shared.

"I was so young. Since I became a single mom at 24, my son Jason and I were as much pals as we were mother and son. I was strict, possibly too strict, but I was going by what Dr. Spock's

book said. I believed in spanking — not hard nor too often —
but he knew I meant business.

"At the same time, Jason got *lots* of love, and I continually built up
his self-confidence, the way my mom had raised me. He thought he
was the greatest kid alive because I told him so every day."

She began smiling as she continued.

"When I started dating after the divorce, guys understood that
we were a 'package deal,' and so Jason went along on lots of
dates with me. I took him lots of places, even during chores like
the grocery store, gift shopping, school shopping — why, he's
run more errands than most people twice his age."

Her eyes twinkled with pride as she talked about her only son.

"I taught him to be nice to everyone, regardless of whether they
were overweight, not the prettiest, or too quiet, because I told
him the people he thought were the geekiest could turn out to
be the most wonderful friends. It paid off for him because he
had many and varied friends by the time he went to high school.

"I made time for us to go to church together, and I listened to
his prayers at night and at mealtime. I could've done more, and
if I had it to do over, I would. But what I did do seems to have
worked. His spiritual side seems to always keep him grounded."

Suzanne paused, sipped her coffee and changed position in her
chair as she continued to reflect.

"Jason also had the benefit of two grandparents (my parents) who saw him almost every day because my mom kept him when he was small. He went over to their house after school most of the time. Because he was given a lot of love from all three of us, he has become a very loving, caring kind of guy."

Suzanne sighed and seemed to be lost in reverie for a few minutes.

I wasn't sure whether I had crossed the line between Suzanne's business and personal life by causing her to share intimate details of her relationship with her son as a single parent, but Suzanne made me feel comfortable by having no hesitation talking about this relationship — and she seemed so proud of Jason.

"Thank you for sharing all that, Suzanne. I can definitely relate. And now that you've told me this, I don't mind sharing with you that I'm struggling with the parental guilt thing. I mean, I love my work and don't want to give it up. Right now, that's not an option anyway. If I could only figure out how to make more quality time at home, maybe that would help.

"I feel lucky having Michael with me because he keeps me from becoming too hard on myself. As I mentioned at an earlier meeting, Michael is more methodical and keeps me grounded — he's not shy about saying how proud of me he is, and he doesn't feel threatened by my advancement. On the other hand, Michael's career is going very well, too, so both of us have to try to keep a balance here...and we often learn from each other."

"I'm so glad you have Michael, Taylor. That sure helps. What are the two of you doing now that helps keep you balanced?"

I laughed out loud. What balance? I thought.

"Okay, let me see. This may sound silly, but I keep the kids' schedule on the fridge so I won't miss something or forget an appointment or a soccer practice."

"That's a good idea. What else?" she asked.

"Well, one thing I insisted on when the babies were born is that we would vow *not* to bring work home. That seemed an easy commitment to keep, but through the years we constantly have to remind each other to *keep work at work*.

"Michael said something to me one time that stuck. He said, 'Taylor, if you constantly have to bring work home, then maybe the job is too big for you.' Oooh, did that ever make me stop and think. It sure caused me to be more productive during work hours so I *didn't* bring it home."

I could feel my face flush.

"That's one way to look at it," Suzanne said. "Unfortunately, there *are* times when you have to bring work home. But Michael is right. Keep work at work as much as you can so your attention goes to the family."

I grumbled agreement. She looked at me expectantly as I went on.

"I believe in parenting on purpose, just like in business. So Michael and I are pretty clear on what we expect at home in terms of chores and routine. This is simply a part of what I'm trying to teach the kids as our family's core values."

"Well said, Taylor!" Now it was Suzanne's turn, and I was ready, pencil in hand. "I find business leaders do the same. They have a focused mission and clearly articulate core values of the organization. It's great to bring those same ideas into family life," Suzanne said. "Good for you!"

"A business leader once shared with me how he and his family developed a mission statement. He had the statement set in type, had multiple prints made...each member of the family signed every print...and framed one for each child's room as well as their kitchen. The mission statement was pretty simple: "Our family loves and supports one another, no matter what." It was a constant reminder that no matter what else was going on in their lives, the mission never changed.

"Periodically, as the children grew older, this same business leader would have family meetings at home — just like we hold in business," she continued. The times were set well in advance, and each person was expected to attend and participate. "Everyone had a vote, although he and his wife reserved the right to veto activities and ideas unsuitable for individual family members or the whole family.

"Sometimes they discussed and voted on vacation destinations.

Other times they talked about family standards and any changes in the ground rules of living in their home.

"Everyone's opinion was respected, every vote counted. Everyone had input, everyone had a platform, and everyone had a hearing when necessary. In most cases, this process of communication headed off problems and kept the family in touch," Suzanne concluded.

"That's a great idea," I agreed, "and I'm always looking for ways to keep on track and in touch at all times. Bottom line, it is not what we leave our kids; it's what we leave within them that counts." I felt strongly about this.

"Taylor, raising a family is a little like being a homebuilder. Building an exceptional house takes lots of forethought before you make the plans and lay the foundation. Things that come later (like plumbing, electricity and communication outlets) are made easier or more difficult depending on how thoroughly the plans and foundation were conceived. So planning ahead will serve you well, and if you've done your job well, you can avoid getting bogged down in any guilt trips.

"When problems arise in your family (and they inevitably will as your children get older), the fact that you and Michael took the time to develop a master plan early on will save much of the grief."

"So did you try to plan your parenting with Jason, Suzanne?" I asked.

"Not at first. I knew I needed some wise counsel just after my divorce. I knew I'd be raising Jason as a single mom, at least for a while, so I went to a few parenting sessions in my community. What I learned helped tremendously with some basic principles I later heard from other mothers and from the counselor:

1. **Respect your family.** As I pursued my career, I kept a steady focus on what is even more important. None of it is worth anything if you don't have people in your life to love and who love you. In my case, that meant Jason, my parents and my extended family. It just never worked out for me to remarry, Taylor. So Jason knew the value of our family as I put first things first. It wasn't always easy. I'd fall asleep sometimes reading to him at night, but that little gesture of bedtime reading was an important part of our routine.

2. **Do what you say.** When I told Jason I would do something, I did *not* take that lightly. I did what I said I'd do. A friend once told the story of a person who had promised her nine-year-old daughter that when she turned ten he would buy her a pony. The mom didn't know of that casual conversation until the day of her daughter's tenth birthday. That little girl cried all night, holding out hope that a pony would be delivered to her front door the next morning. Kids don't forget, and neither should we! Believe me, after that story I was careful what I promised Jason. In turn, he learned to follow through on commitments.

3. **Set goals.** One mom said every New Year's she and her husband and their kids would pop popcorn and watch movies before writing down their goals for the coming year. Then they'd take the previous year's lists from a special hiding place and review how they'd all done. The kids got to check up on what their parents had accomplished, as well as the parents keeping track of the kids.

4. **Make home a special place.** "I made sure our house was always a place that Jason *wanted* to be, not just the place he had to go to every day after school. As a result, it was also a place his friends wanted to be. I guess it's because I let them be who they were — not that I let them get away with things — and didn't bother them or get in their business too much. In our home we had fun and laughed a lot. Some of his friends would come over even when Jason wasn't home and just visit with me. At times I felt like I was never alone, but that's certainly better than wondering where your child is and what he's up to."

Suzanne continued: "Taylor, here's the good news in all this. Being a mom is a great school for managers. Seriously, motherhood actually requires highly efficient management skills: it demands organization, listening, pacing, coaching and guiding, leading, monitoring, handling conflict and imparting information.

"The ability to tolerate ambiguity and to multitask well is often attributed to women as a vital but often underrated management skill. So use your incredible strengths, Taylor. And just go for it."

I loved her positive attitude, and I certainly needed the encouragement. She was right. I wasn't doing so bad after all. You do what you have to do, as they say.

With a sigh of relief I turned to Suzanne and said, "You've raised a son and can relate to my desire to have a balanced life. But the reality is, there's no such perfection. I have to be flexible with whatever comes. Isn't that it?" I asked without waiting for a response. "If someone had figured out a way to have the balanced life, there would be reams of books giving the answers.

"I can never thank you enough, Suzanne," I said. "You make it look simple, and you've provided step-by-step suggestions as we've gone along, so I know I can do this. And I'll share with Michael all you said about the family. I know he'll appreciate your thoughts. Let's get to work."

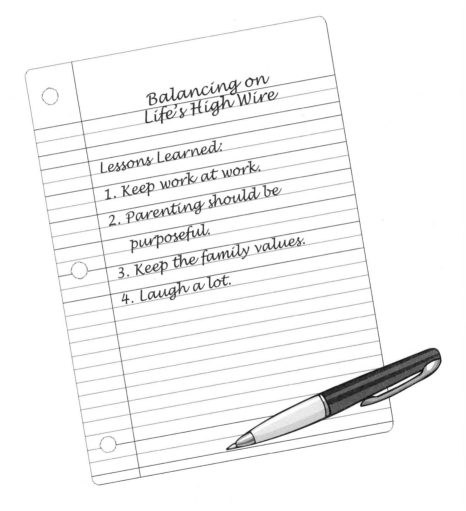

Balancing on
Life's High Wire

Lessons Learned:
1. Keep work at work.
2. Parenting should be purposeful.
3. Keep the family values.
4. Laugh a lot.

The Eighth Monday

Helping Others Become The Obvious Choice

*I*t had been two weeks since our last meeting. Suzanne had called to let me know that something had come up unexpectedly last Monday. Now I knew what it was!

The buzz at yoga last week was about Suzanne's organization being recognized as one of the city's "best places to work." The newspaper article featured my mentor being named the managing partner of her firm. What an honor for her, and what a privilege for me to have such a special relationship with someone so capable.

Excitedly, I drove the few miles from my house to our favorite coffee shop. I was really going to miss these Monday mornings with Suzanne. Michael and I had reflected over the weekend how much I had gained from our meetings. Suzanne had given me relevant guidance on better ways to manage my team and myself. Over and over it was apparent that these sessions had at times given me new insights; at other times Suzanne simply listened and confirmed that my thoughts were not silly — that even she had experienced some of the same doubts and frustrations throughout her career.

Michael, being the caring husband that he is, reflected that I seemed much calmer and more in control of the pressures at work. We both were grateful for that! It's hard to avoid bringing those emotional pressures home. I certainly felt better, and I was enjoying time with my boys in the evenings like I used to. It meant a lot to hear Michael confirm I was making progress!

He was especially glad to hear Suzanne's comments last week as we talked about purposeful parenting. He also agreed wholeheartedly that raising our family with values and commitments was key to building a happy home. We even created our own family mission statement.

Once again, I was glad that we both agreed on how we wanted to raise Mason and Josh — on how important it was to lay a strong foundation for them. Suzanne's advice to laugh a lot was easy in our family. Michael has a great sense of humor that keeps me seeing the light side of things when I might easily get down on myself.

With a thank-you gift for Suzanne in my hand, I walked into Starbucks looking right at the corner area, hoping our favorite chairs were waiting for us. She was already seated and had a big smile on her face. How classy she looked this morning in a trendy yet smart black suit and crisp white shirt. That was the "power look," I had been told.

Suzanne rose from her seat to greet me with a hug this morning. All smiles, she said, "Good morning, Taylor. Here we are at our last meeting with so much left to talk about."

Before she had a chance to say anything else, I blurted out, "Hey, congratulations to you! The article about your firm was great. I can't wait to hear about it. Watch my things while I get a cup of coffee."

Suzanne was beaming. What great news for discussion during our last session. I wanted to spend the whole hour just hearing about it. Hurrying back to our spot, I was ready to listen.

"So fill me in, Suzanne. I want to hear all your news."

Having a work environment like Suzanne's was something I wanted for my organization. Her guidance had already helped me see things I could do at my level to have the same environment. Now I couldn't wait to get the inside scoop on her promotion.

She leaned forward, wriggling in her chair with cheerful energy.

"We're all excited, of course," she began. "And clearly our success has taken lots of effort from lots of people. It sure didn't happen overnight," she said humbly." She paused and with a smile added, "It *was* a nice article in the paper, wasn't it?"

"Yes, and everyone at yoga class is really proud of you," I replied as I reached to pick up her gift.

"I have something for you, Suzanne. Open it now, ok?" I couldn't wait to give it to her.

As she opened the framed picture of the newspaper article featuring her as the head of the firm, the expression on her face showed me how much she liked it.

"Taylor, you couldn't have given me anything more special. What a nice gift. I'll keep it in my office to remind me of our friendship. Thank you so much."

Her tone of voice lowered as she began talking about her company.

"It is a group effort, like I said. And I'm delighted several of us received promotions last week. That's why I was so tied up and couldn't meet with you last Monday."

"I certainly understand. So what's your first challenge in your new role?" I wanted to know all about it.

"I think I'll spend time meeting with people at every level in an effort to help them understand my vision and commitment for the future. Doing this also gives me an opportunity to get feedback. That's important to me, Taylor — getting everyone on board and letting them know each one is a valued contributor. So that's my first goal. Now, what about you? What would you like to talk about this morning?" She refocused to her role as my mentor.

"Actually, this is a good topic for me, Suzanne. I want to help my people move forward in their careers, but I'm not sure exactly how to do that. There's one man in particular I'd love to see promoted. Frank has been around a few years longer than I have. He's really good at what he does, but he's quiet, and no one knows him very well. How involved should I get in helping him?"

I wanted to know whether people should be in charge of their own careers or whether I, as their manager, had a role to play in helping them.

"Have you asked Frank if he's interested in getting promoted? Some people are happy in their jobs and don't want to move into management. And that's ok. We need strong followers just as we need people who strive to advance into leadership roles," Suzanne clearly stated.

"Yes," I replied. "I asked Frank just the other day what his aspirations are. He said he'd like to become a manager and felt like he should be recognized for his work without having to tout his talents — those were his words," I said.

"You and I know that's not the case, Taylor. You were promoted to management because you took advantage of opportunities and made the most of them. You gained exposure and recognition as a result, right?"

Suzanne continued to ask questions.

"Some people feel like their efforts alone will get recognition. But that's not enough. Remember the discussion we had about managing sideways, up and down in your organization? Well, Frank has to be able to manage up and get people above him to think of him as a leader. He has to leave his comfort zone and stretch to the next level. Sometimes people have to be pulled along the way.

"Let's think of ways Frank can get exposure to upper management so he can make himself the obvious choice for the next promotion."

She suggested, "What about giving him opportunities to make some presentations to your boss or even higher management?"

"He's quiet, though, Suzanne. I don't want to put him on the spot. On the other hand, nothing ventured, nothing gained. So I'll ask him!"

"All you can do is offer him the opportunities, Taylor. He's got to take the action.

"Keep in mind that most of us have anxiety when giving presentations. He'll never grow if you don't afford him the opportunity. You could certainly help him with his presentations. Remember when you told me the lessons you learned in your childhood? Some of them were about how easy it was for you to present in front of people — that you actually liked it. So work with him on his speaking. I'd also send him to a presentation skills course. There are lots of them around, Taylor. Anyone in a management role needs to be able to make effective presentations and get past the stage fright."

Suzanne was right. I enjoyed making presentations. Why shouldn't I help Frank and anyone else on my team? Communication was a leadership competency that came easily for me, and Suzanne had told me earlier to pass leadership lessons on. This could be my first chance to do just that!

"Any other suggestions, Suzanne?" I probed. "What else could Frank do to gain recognition from the top and become the obvious choice when an opportunity arises?"

"How about giving Frank a project that has significant impact up in the organization? Wanting to lead isn't enough, Taylor. Frank has to show himself as a leader," she said emphatically.

I thought of an idea. "You're right," I said. "As a matter of fact, he might enjoy a project that I have on my plate right now. For the past several years I've been in charge of our annual customer satisfaction meeting. Each year we bring in twenty to thirty key customers for a formal meeting to gain their insights and to hear their opinions on our products and services. Last year we announced five new products. These customers gave us great input as we launched all five of them. Four of the five are selling well; however, one is lagging. Maybe this year we can find out some reasons why.

"No one understands the market better than our customers. So this year we want to bring in our top ten customers as a focus group. They'll sign a nondisclosure agreement in order for us to share our ideas for next year's new products to see how receptive they'll be to what we're planning. It's amazing what we learn when we listen to our customers. Typically I would spend a large amount of time planning, preparing, executing and managing this meeting. But this is perfect for Frank. It would also be a growing experience for me because I will have to let go and trust Frank and his ability to carry it off to my standards."

Suzanne warned, "Don't forget, Taylor. **Never expect what you don't inspect.** Learning to delegate is a good rule, but what you can never delegate is your accountability. The results will still reside with you. Learning how to macro-manage with micro understanding is critical to your project. It's my belief that management is an art, not a science."

I agreed and said, "Frank is excellent at handling details, so this should be right up his alley. And our senior management always attends the meeting, so he'll be able to gain exposure and recognition. Perfect, Suzanne. I can't wait to get back and talk with him. I know he could rise to the occasion with my support."

"Another thing, Taylor. One of your responsibilities as a leader is to always be focused on getting your top 10 percent promoted. If you help Frank become the obvious choice for the next promotion, others will see opportunities they can take advantage of."

Suzanne shared with me her belief that as a manager my **success**

is measured not by how I am doing, but how well my people are doing.

"You know, Taylor, I have great satisfaction with the promotion I just received," she said humbly, "and I know it's based on the fact that my team performed well. I can now step into this new role and know that the area of responsibility I left behind will function and not miss a beat. If I had to point to one thing that got me this promotion, it would be that I never lost sight of the fact that if my people did well, I would do well and be recognized."

Hesitantly, I glanced at my watch, knowing our time was up. I bluntly said, "Suzanne, I just hate to have this end. I know we can't meet every Monday anymore, but I hope we can get together from time to time and have a cup of coffee. I still want to reserve the right to call you when I have a question, because I value your input."

"Why don't we have a signal?" she said understandingly. "You can give me an 811 call that lets me know if you really need my advice, Taylor. If you leave a voice mail that says you're making an 811 call, I'll know to get back with you as soon as I can. Would that work?"

"Absolutely, and thank you so much for making yourself available to me. I promise not to make it a habit to call unless I'm stuck on an issue," I assured her.

"Look, Taylor," she said purposefully. "I've thoroughly enjoyed our relationship, and I don't intend to be a stranger."

As we gathered our things to leave the table, she continued, "So coffee is a certain, and I'll always be a good listener and contributor when I can. One of the things I've admired about you is that you have taken our conversations to heart each week and tried to apply what we've discussed. It's been rewarding watching you grow, and I fully expect you to have a job at my level some day. Don't think I haven't learned from you as well. It's been fun seeing your enthusiasm and positive attitude. Just remember that cream always rises to the top...and you're cream, Taylor."

We hugged and walked out together. Just as I was about to turn toward my car, she quickly lifted from her purse a small package and handed it to me with a warm smile.

"Now it's my turn to give you something, Taylor."

I was totally surprised and couldn't help but choke back tears as I opened the box to find a sterling silver key chain in it — simple and elegant.

"This is to remind you of key leadership lessons you have already learned and other lessons you'll continue to learn. Managing people is a long-term learning experience. But leadership is really pretty simple. It's like the acronym **K.I.S.S., which means 'keep it straightforward and simple.'** As long as you keep your positive attitude and shoot straight with people, they'll work hard for you because they'll trust you. As long as people trust you, their productivity will be strong."

Suzanne paused, and I realized the bond we had established in such a short time.

I thanked my mentor one more time as we said our goodbyes, promising to stay in touch. As I drove to my office, I knew we would stay connected. And that made me happy!

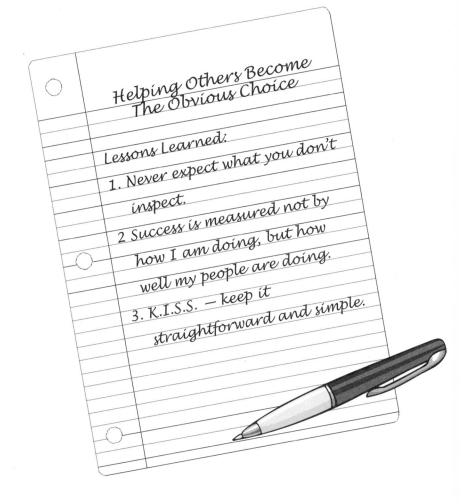

Helping Others Become
The Obvious Choice

Lessons Learned:
1. Never expect what you don't inspect.
2 Success is measured not by how I am doing, but how well my people are doing.
3. K.I.S.S. — keep it straightforward and simple.

Epilogue

*I*t's been two years since those eight Monday mornings with Suzanne Chambers. I still carry her key chain as a constant reminder of the impact she made in my career and my life. We meet once in a while for a cup of coffee, sometimes to talk about important issues that come up and other times just to catch up personally.

Suzanne was right about leadership; there are always challenges when managing others. But her advice has worked for me.

In the past two years, here's what's happened:

My boys, Mason and Josh, are now in the third and fifth grades. They're really doing well, and I'm enjoying them more every day. Michael lost his job due to a merger and has launched himself into a new career. The start-up has been tough, but he's happy with the transition. I really admire the way he handled the unexpected change in his career...I think that Suzanne's advice to me had a positive impact on him as well.

I have a new position in our organization with more responsibility and more direct reports. I have been so blessed. Our merger was successful, and Doug remained my boss until he retired this year. I am still in the process of "breaking in" my new manager. He's not used to someone like me managing up, so it's a transition for both of us. I still have to remind myself of one of Suzanne's first words of advice...patience, Taylor.

Brandon and I have developed a strong business relationship. He's been supportive through thick and thin. Believe it or not, timeliness is now his virtue. He's shown me the importance and results of managing sideways.

Hiring tough continues to be a challenge, but one that pays high dividends. I've hired six people over the past two years, and four of those new hires have strengthened my new team. One I had to let go almost immediately and the other is making progress. I am still trying to perfect the "hire tough so I can manage easy" concept.

Frank was promoted six months ago and is flourishing in his management role. He joined Toastmasters and is now one of the best presenters in the organization. I'm proud of his success... There's no greater satisfaction that a manager can receive than seeing one of the team thrive with the challenges of a new opportunity.

And extremely important to me is that I am now mentoring Karen Pearce. She is a chief nursing officer at a local hospital.

I've found that the lessons I learned apply to women in all walks of life. We meet at Starbucks every Monday.

I am so grateful to give back what I received from my wonderful mentor, Suzanne. Many of you who have read this book will do the same.

I wish you the best.

Wisdom from Suzanne
A Collection of Quotations

"Leadership has to be earned.
The long and short of it…it takes time."
Page 20

"Hold only meetings that are absolutely necessary,
meetings that give your team something to make their jobs easier
or tips to make them more effective employees."
Page 37

"Some people think differently from you and communicate differently.
It doesn't make your style right or wrong – just different."
Page 47

"Do unto others as they would like you to do unto them."
Page 49

"We need to be shifting our thinking on how we
must work across the organization –
from west to east – rather than from the top down."
Page 59

"We are living in a world of raplexity –
a business environment that changes rapidly,
and, as changes occur, they are more and more complex."
Page 67

"There's nothing wrong with honestly saying, 'I don't know.'"
Page 68

*"Do the right things rather than hammer
on doing things exactly right."*
Page 75

"Keep the main thing the main thing."
Page 76

*"Staff to your weaknesses so you can
focus on your areas of strength."*
Page 87

*"It is not what we leave our kids;
it's what we leave within them that counts."*
Page 99

"Being a mom is a great school for managers."
Page 101

*"As long as you keep your positive attitude and shoot straight with
people, most will work hard for you because they'll trust you."*
Page 114

Acknowledgements

When I finished this book and began writing acknowledgments, it became obvious to me how many people have impacted my career and achievements. I'm grateful for each one's talents and mentoring in different stages of my life. Each person gave willingly of his or her time to take me to new heights personally and professionally.

First and foremost I'm blessed to have my beloved husband and partner, Doug, as the greatest mentor any woman could have. He continues to be my role model for every principle in this book. Mentoring behind the scenes has allowed me to grow in so many ways.

A huge thanks to David Cottrell, Cornerstone Leadership, for offering me the opportunity to publish this book. His enthusiasm and contagious energy kept me focused.

A special thanks to clients including Verizon, Mary Kay, Microsoft, Chugai Pharma and Texas Guaranteed who continue to use our leadership training and consulting to improve their organizations. Thanks also to the Pritchett organization for the intellectual capitol gained over my past twelve years of affiliation.

Lastly, thanks to our daughter Stephanie Taylor who never tired of reading the script as a work in progress. I always value her opinion.

About the Author

Valerie Sokolosky, is President of Valerie & Company, an international leadership development company in Dallas, TX. The firm's expertise has received front-page Wall Street Journal press coverage. For over 25 years, Valerie has influenced the corporate world as an international keynote speaker and author  of seven books. Known for her high energy and impactful presentations, Valerie has helped thousands reach their leadership potential using practical tips and poignant stories.

She currently serves on the Board of the prestigious organization Leadership America and has written monthly articles for SW Airlines Magazine for the past seven years.

Valerie has been honored as Delta Zeta Woman of the Year, participated in M.I.T. President's Forum, member of Executive Women of Dallas and committee chairman for St. Jude's Research Hospital Charity Event.

Her client list includes Alfa Corporativo and Cemex-Mexico, Verizon, Neiman-Marcus, Avon, Mary Kay, Microsoft, Texaco, Shell Oil, Dell Computers, Pfizer, Chugai Pharma, EDS, Motorola, American Airlines, British Airways, and American Express among others.

For more information about Valerie & Company, please visit www.**valerieandcompany**.com.

To book Valerie Sokolosky for a *Monday Morning Leadership for Women* speaking engagement, please contact:
Barbara Bartlett
CornerStone Leadership Institute
888.789.5323

Other CornerStone Leadership Books

Monday Morning Leadership is David Cottrell's newest and best-selling book. It offers unique encouragement and direction that will help you become a better manager, employee, and person. **$12.95**

Listen Up, Leader! Ever wonder what employees think about their leaders? This book tells you the seven characteristics of leadership that people will follow. **$9.95**

Walk the Talk...And Get the Results You Want is a compelling allegory showing how to bring new life to your organization and turn values and ethics into value-added results. **$21.95**

The Manager's Coaching Handbook is a practical guide to improve performance from your superstars, middle stars and falling stars. **$9.95**

Sticking To It: The Art of Adherence reveals the secret to success for high achieving organizations and provides practical advice on how you can win the game of business. **$9.95**

Ethics 4 Everyone provides practical information to guide individual actions, decisions, and daily behaviors. **$9.95**

175 Ways to Get More Done in Less Time has 175 really, really good suggestions that will help you get things done faster...usually better. **$9.95**

180 Ways to Walk the Recognition Talk is packed with proven techniques and practical strategies that will help you encourage positive, productive performance. **$9.95**

136 Effective Presentation Tips is a powerful handbook providing 136 practical, easy to use tips to make every presentation a success. **$9.95**

Becoming the Obvious Choice is a roadmap showing each employee how they can maintain their motivation, develop their hidden talents, and become the best. **$9.95**

Nuts 'n Bolts provides practical, easy to follow "how to's" to help your people meet their most challenging leadership responsibilities. **$9.95**

Manager's Communication Handbook will allow you to connect with employees and create the understanding, support and acceptance critical to your success. **$9.95**

The Secrets of Meeting Magic Revealed is full of key ideas, strategies, and tested processes that will drive big improvements in the meeting you lead or attend. **$9.95**

Management Insights explores the myths and realities of management. It provides insight into how you can become a successful manager. **$14.95**

Leading to Ethics provides you with the tools to meet the responsibility of building an integrity and values-based organization. **$9.95**

Goal Setting for Results addresses the fundamentals of setting and achieving your goal of moving yourself and your organization from where you are, to where you want (and need) to be! **$9.95**

The Leadership Secrets of Santa Claus: How To Get Big Things Done in Your "Workshop"...All Year Long is the perfect gift for leaders at ALL levels to help them accomplish "big things" by giving employees clear goals, solid accountabilities, ongoing feedback, coaching, and recognition in your "workshop". **$12.95**

Back to Basics...Tried and True Solutios for Today's Leaders 32 members of the ADL Associates network share some of the best "basic" ideas and strategies that are the core of an organization's success. **$9.95**

Recommended Resources for Additional Study:

From Steamroller to Leader
> *Listen Up, Leader! Pay Attention, Improve and Guide*

Rocks, Pebbles, Sand and Water
> *175 Ways to Get More Done in Less Time*

The Platinum Rule
> *Walk the Talk...And Get The Results You Want*

Managing Sideways
> *The Manager's Communication Handbook*

Living in Raplexity
> *Sticking to It: The Art of Adherence*

Hire Tough
> *The Managers Coaching Handbook: A Practical Guide to Improving Employee Performance*

Balancing on Life's High Wire
> *Monday Morning Leadership: 8 Mentoring Sessions You Can't Afford to Miss*

Helping Others Become the Obvious Choice
> *Becoming the Obvious Choice: A Guide to Your Next Opportunity*

To order these recommended resources,
call 1-888-789-5323 or
visit www.**cornerstoneleadership**.com

☑ YES! Please send me extra copies of *Monday Morning Leadership for Women!*
  1-30 copies $14.95   31-100 copies $13.95   100+ copies $12.95

Monday Morning Leadership for Women	____ copies X _____	= $_____
Monday Morning Leadership for Women **Audio CD**	____ copies X $19.95	= $_____
Monday Morning Leadership **Audio CD**	____ copies X $19.95	= $_____

Additional Leadership Development Books

Listen Up, Leader!	____ copies X $9.95	= $_____
175 Ways to Get More Done in Less Time	____ copies X $9.95	= $_____
Walk the Talk…And Get The Results You Want	____ copies X $21.95	= $_____
The Manager's Communication Handbook	____ copies X $9.95	= $_____
Sticking to It: The Art of Adherence	____ copies X $9.95	= $_____
The Manager's Coaching Handbook	____ copies X $9.95	= $_____
Monday Morning Leadership	____ copies X $12.95	= $_____
Becoming the Obvious Choice	____ copies X $9.95	= $_____
180 Ways to Walk the Recognition Talk	____ copies X $9.95	= $_____
136 Effective Presentation Tips	____ copies X $9.95	= $_____
Leadership Development Package (one of each of the 10 books above)	____ packs X $99.95	= $_____
	Shipping & Handling	$_____
	Subtotal	$_____
	Sales Tax (8.25%-TX Only)	$_____
	Total (U.S. Dollars Only)	**$_____**

Shipping and Handling Charges

Total $ Amount	Up to $50	$51-$99	$100-$249	$250-$1199	$1200-$3000	$3000+
Charge	$5	$8	$16	$30	$80	$125

Name _____ Job Title _____

Organization _____ Phone _____

Shipping Address _____ Fax _____

Billing Address _____ Email _____

City _____ State _____ Zip _____

❑ Please invoice (Orders over $200) Purchase Order Number (if applicable) _____

Charge Your Order: ❑ MasterCard   ❑ Visa   ❑ American Express

Credit Card Number _____ Exp. Date _____

Signature _____

❑ Check Enclosed (Payable to CornerStone Leadership)

Fax: 972.274.2884   **Mail: P.O. Box 764087**   **Phone: 888.789.5323**
Dallas, TX 75376
www.**cornerstoneleadership**.com

CornerStone
Leadership Institute

www.**cornerstoneleadership**.com